Wood Pellet Smoker Grill Cookbook

By

Aron Smith

Table of Contents

Introduction

What's not to love about smoked meat? They're God's gift to man, as far as I'm concerned. Ever so tender, so moist, so spicy, juicy, and wonderfully smoky! You could never accuse smoked meats of not having flavor, that's for sure. When they're done right, that is.

Now, the process of smoking meat can be pretty intimidating if you don't know what to do, but I've got to tell you, it's worth it. Especially when you're using a wood pellet smoker grill. Now I've got to tell you, grilled meals are awesome, but if you want the highest quality of grilled meats, then you can do no better than a wood pellet smoker grill.

You see, when you deal with electric smokers, there are so many limitations you have to contend with. There's only so much you can do. But when you've got a wood pellet smoker grill, then you'll find there's a whole new world of food out there, open for you to explore. I guarantee if you've been using electric grills, and then you decide to switch over to wood pellet smoker grills, you will never even dream of going back. You and your grill will be going steady till the day you croak, I guarantee it. You can use your wood pellet smoker grill not just for grilling, but for baking, and roasting as well.

As you prepare your meals using your wood pellet smoker grill, you'll find it near impossible not to be swamped with lots of requests from family and friends to prepare this, that, and the other meal. Home cooked meals will suddenly trump anything you could get at the fanciest restaurant you know. That's a good thing, too, since you're the one making your own meals, so you'll know what's in it.

In this book, I'm going to give you a bunch of recipes that will simply blow your mind, reconstruct it, and then blow it again. You're wondering if they're that good. Well, I'm **telling** you they **are** that awesome! Just keep in mind as you read that nothing here is set in stone. If you've got an idea on how you can tweak stuff, then just go for it! After all, the best recipes exist because someone decided to experiment. How do you think cream soda was created? Or cereal? There you go. Have fun with this!

You might hear a wood pellet smoker and grill being called a pellet grill, pellet smoker, or pellet smoker grill. Keep in mind it's all the same thing, okay?

Chapter One: The Basics

Before we sink our teeth into the juicy recipes lined up in this book, we've simply got to talk about the basics. So let's begin!

Barbecue

You've no doubt heard the term, even if you've somehow never(?!) had any before. Barbecuing is a method of cooking, and is probably the oldest method ever. When you barbecue stuff, you can't go wrong with the low-and-slow method, using indirect heat to smoke your meats and other stuff. Besides the heat which cooks your food indirectly, you've for the smoke, rubs, spices, and the juice which is naturally in the meat. That's it.

You may have heard people use the terms "barbecue" and "grilling" interchangeably, but there is a huge difference! Just because you're making some hot dogs or cooking some chicken on hot coal or with some other type of grill does not automatically mean you're making barbecue **anything.**

That's not to say you cannot make barbecue meals using some hot coal and indirect heat as well. We could get into the whole argument of what that's really about, but I'll just save it for another book. All you need to know is that your wood pellet smoker grill is the best thing ever for barbecue. Point, blank, period.

The Wood Pellet Smoker Grill

The wood pellet smoker grill is a barbecue pt. It uses hardwood sawdust which has been compressed, like hickory, mesquite, oak, cherry, and apple, among other kinds of wood pellets, to grill, roast, bake, and smoke your food. The thing about the wood pellet smoker grill is that it gives you a very complex, rich flavor profile, and also the perfect amount of moisture which you could never get with any other method of cooking. The temperatures of the grill can range from 150 degrees Fahrenheit to way beyond 600 degrees Fahrenheit, depending on the make and model. You'll be happy to know you can do all the searing and grilling you want to on a wood pellet smoker grill.

Among all the many awesome features of the modern day wood pellet smoker grill, you're going to love the fact that they are convenient, give all the succulent juiciness you want in your meats, and excel far beyond other coal and gas grills when it comes to safety. I should state right off the bat that the smoke profile is nowhere near as wild as all the other smokers you've used in the past. The wood pellet smoker grill is deliberately designed to allow you to work with it in whichever way you desire, and also serve as a convection oven if you need one.

Best of all, they are incredibly simple to run! You don't need to go get a degree in rocket science before you know how to work your wood pellet smoker grill. That said, let's talk about the basic parts of a wood pellet smoker grill.

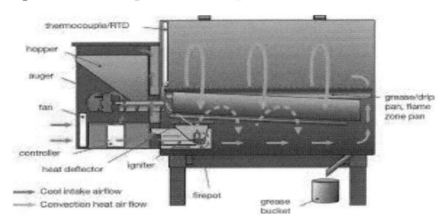

Parts of A Wood Pellet Smoker Grill

We're going to go over all the parts of a wood pellet smoker grill, so you know what you're working with when you get your own. Let's get into it.

The Hopper. You'll be keeping your wood pellets here. When you store your wood pellets, you want to make sure you've got just enough in there to take you through the length of time you'll need for cooking, give you the temperature you need, and meet the capacity recommended for your hopper.

The Auger. The pellets are delivered to the fire pot through the auger.

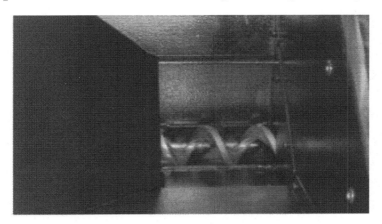

The Fire Pot. The fire pot is where the pellets go. With the fire pot, you can ignite the wood pellets which will then heat up the grill. You will find there's a big hold in the fire pot. This hole is where you connect the pellet tube. The pellet tube also has the auger in it, so you can feed the pellets directly to the pot. In the fire pot, there is an even bigger hole in the lower, in the middle. This other hole is specifically for connecting the igniter rod. Every other hole in the fire pot is to allow airflow from the fan. You want to always make sure you empty out all the ashes after a few cooking sessions. If you don't do this, then you'll find the igniter won't work as well as it used to over time. You could also vacuum the ashes out as well, if you like.

The Igniter Rod/Element. This is what lights up the wood pellets which are in the fire pot. When you remove the fire pot, you'll be able to see the igniter rod as well as the pellet feed tube which feeds pellets to the fire pot through the auger.

The Fan. This keeps the airflow constant or dynamic, depending on what you're going for. Thanks to the fan, the pellets continue burning, making convection cooking a breeze.

The Thermocouple/Resistive Temperature Detector (RTD). This thermal sensor gives the controller the feedback loop. You must make sure that you always keep the thermocouple clean by wiping it down after a number of cooking sessions. When you do this, you can be assured of more accurate heat measurements.

The Heat Deflector. Just as the name suggests, the heat deflector is what helps absorb heat. It also helps the heat spread out nice and even underneath the drip pan, so that your wood pellet smoker grill functions as a convection open. You'll find the head deflector covering the fire pot.

The Drip/Grease Pan. You can use this part of your wood pellet smoker grill for smoking, roasting, baking, and indirect cooking as well. What the pan does is to help move the grease which you'll get naturally from cooking, right to grease bucket. Now make sure that you always get rid of all residue after each cooking session. Scrape it off to keep it nice and clean. I cannot stress enough that you should make use of foil. If you do, make sure you change the foil after every few cooking sessions.

The Flame Zone Pan. This is used for grilling directly, at really high temperatures. More often than not, you'll find it being used alongside searing grates, and other griddle accessories.

The Controller. You'll find that there are many forms in which the controller comes. It's function is simple. With the controller, you can adjust the airflow and pellet flow so the temperature you desire remains consistent.

The Grease Bucket. This is what collects all the grease and fat as you cook your yummy meats. Grease definitely will accumulate over time. The amount that does accumulate will depend on the way you handle trimming excess fat and fat caps from poultry and meat. If you would like your clean up sessions to be a breeze, then you definitely should consider lining the bucket with foil. You may then discard all the grease in empty cans, which you can then toss in the trash.

Reasons You Should Switch to A Wood Pellet Smoker Grill

The wood pellet smoker grill is the absolute best choice you could make when it comes to all your grilling and barbecue needs. You'll find that you won't have to keep buying replacement grills with each new season, and you won't need more than one of them.

With the wood pellet smoker grill, you can do low and slow cooking, smoke, bake, roast, and grill. Not unlike propane grills, you can get it all preheated in a matter of 10 minutes to 15 minutes, tops. Flare-ups are a thing of the past, as are the ridiculously harsh flavors from the smoke you get from charcoal or wood.

Why else should you make the switch to the wood pellet smoker grill, besides incredibly moist and tasty meals? You'll find that they are super easy to work, and just as easy to maintain as well. Best of all, everything runs automatically. You just need to keep your hopper full of enough wood pellets, and then hook up that bad boy to a power source, and you're good to go. In the whole contraption, you can only move the fan and the auger.

When it comes to other types of grilling units, you'll need to keep track of so much more than just those two parts. When it comes to other kinds of smoker grills, you have to constantly keep track of every part of the unit, if you're going to get a steady temp going. However, the woo pellet smoker grill is designed in such a way that your temperature stays at whatever level you set it to. The steady temperature means you can actually smoke stuff like seafood, and poultry without ruining it, since you need the temperatures to be low enough to generate the perfect amount of smoke.

The Perfect Temperature

For you to achieve the perfect temperature, you've got to be able to control your grill. The wood pellet smoker grill lets you do just that, with the controller, which adjusts both the flow of pellets and air, so that the temperature you've chosen remains constant. You should keep in mind that some manufacturers create their own controllers, while others enlist the services of a third party. Either way, it helps to be able to tell which controller is which. You want the kind that makes it possible to precisely set and control the temperature of your wood pellet smoker grill. You'll find that there are three kinds of controllers:

Analog Controllers. These are your standard units. They'll typically give you exactly three temperature set points: Low, medium, and high, also known as LMH. The entry level wood pellet smoker grills are the ones which come with this sort of controller.

You're not likely to find a thermocouple temperature probe or an RTD which could play the part of giving the feedback loop.

I shouldn't have to point out that analog controllers are far from the best sort. The temperature fluctuates a lot when you use them, and it doesn't self-correct when it comes to ambient temperatures. All you can do is set the timer for turning the auger on and off, for the low, medium, and high temperatures, which are already preset by the manufacturer. Could there be a better option?

Digital Controllers. These controllers are better than the analog controllers in that they actually have an RTD temperature probe, which gives you that much needed feedback loop for flawless cooking. You'll find that most of the digital controllers out there have an increment setting of 25 degrees Fahrenheit. Once you've got the RTD temperature probe installed, you can have an even better substitute for the analog, LMH controllers. It pretty much works like your standard home thermostat.

All you have to do is enter your preset temperature, and once that is reached, the controller will switch the auger on for a set number of seconds, then off again for a set number of seconds. Next, it idles for a bit, unless the temperature deviates from your preset number. Once that happens, the cycle repeats itself. There are some digital controllers which will let you set up how long you want your unit to idle for. That way, ambient temperatures are accounted for.

Proportional Integral Derivative Controllers. Also known as PID controllers, these bad boys are the best value for your money. They are more advanced than the analog and digital controllers, which means even better temperature control for you. They have a thermocouple temperature probe with a control loop feedback, which helps to consistently check the temperature you want against the current temperature; then it makes the required adjustments.

With a PID controller, you have the option of setting cooking temperature in increments of 5 degrees. The auger feed rate can also be adjusted using the controller, and more often than not, there will be a variable number of fan speed settings, which help greatly in keeping the temperature stable, always keeping it within no more than 5 degrees Fahrenheit of the temperature you've set. What this means is when it comes to controlling temperature, it really doesn't get better than the PID controller.

You'll find that the best wood pellet smoker grills have a PID controller already installed, and run by the most sophisticated programming to give you the precision you need. There are even control systems which have two or more meat temperature probes, and have even more settings which give you the flexibility you need for cooking.

All that said, the absolute least you should settle for when it comes to getting a wood pellet smoker grill is the kind with a digital controller. If you can get a PID controller, that would be even better.

The Origin of The Wood Pellet Smoker Grill

If you're wondering who you have to thank for the wonder that is the wood pellet smoker grill, it's this little company in Oregon which was called Traeger Hills. That's the company that came up with the wood pellet smoker grill in the 1990s.

Ever since then, that industry has grown exponentially, especially after the patent held by Traeger expired. It was only a matter of time before word of the wood pellet smoker grill would spread far and wide, and everyone wanted their very own, so they could enjoy delicious meals. Where it was once only Traager making wood pellet smoker grills, now you've got other manufacturers such as MAK, which happens to be in Oregon as well.

Today, you're going to find over a score of the best wood pellet smoker grill makes everywhere, whether it's your barbecue store, or your hardware store, or online, or in a regular brick and mortar store. You also have the option of getting yours straight from the manufacturer, too. From entry level units, to the sleeker, state of the art units, you'll find that they go from as low as $300 to as high as $2,500 or even more.

Assembling Your Wood Pellet Smoker Grill

If your dealer has not already assisted you with assembling your unit, then you'll need to do it yourself. Don't worry, I've got you covered. Also, it's really not rocket science. All you've got to do is set out all the parts, and be sure to go through the accompanying instruction manual before you attempt to assemble your unit. If you get lost or confused, you could always hit up tech support to assist you over the phone. Thankfully, manufacturers offer customer support. The good ones, anyway.

If you follow the instructions to the letter, you should have no problem putting your unit together in under an hour. For the most part, units will usually only require you to put the legs and the base in. Do note that if the instructions explicitly state you'll need two people to assemble it, then you should definitely get someone to help you out so you do not hurt yourself, okay?

The Ignition

Most wood pellet smoker grills make use of the standard 120 VAC outlets, or the 12 VDC outlets which you'll find at home. There are some units which will need 12 VDC from a deep cycle battery, or a car battery. All in all, your wood pellet smoker grill very likely doesn't need all that much, when it comes to power. All that will actually be powered in your unit are the an, igniter rod, auger, and controller.

Still on the ignition, you never have to worry about the wood pellet smoker grill being unsafe. All the fire stays in the fire pot, and event that is completely covered by the grease pan. Translation: You don't have to worry about flare-ups. Once you power up your unit you're either going to have the pit power up sequentially, or it will follow a different order of events, depending on your manufacturer.

Once the controller goes on, the igniter rod will also go on. You can tell when the rod is on, because it will be red hot, literally glowing. Then the auger funnels a particular amount of pellets straight into the fire pot, while the fan sends the air moving through the smaller holes which we talked about into the fire pot as well, causing the fire to start, and to remain steady.

The igniter rod will then either go off after a period of time — usually four minutes or more — or it will go off when the pit has achieved the preset temperature. Remember, if it's a PID controller, the igniter rod will be switched back on whenever the temperature happens to dip below your preferred temperature. This way, you don't have to deal with annoying flameouts.

The Burn In Procedure

The reason for doing the burn in procedure before you begin cooking with your wood pellet smoker grill is because you want to make sure all the contaminants from the manufacturing process, as well as any oils, are all gone. You don't want to cook something right away and have it tasting like it was also manufactured. =

So before anything else, the first thing you want to do is stock your hopper with some hardwood wood pellets. Make sure they are barbecue grade, and nothing less. Now, it might take your auger a little more than ten minutes to get the first of the pellets into the fire pot, so go ahead and put the pellets in yourself, directly. All you need is half a handful, nothing more.

Next, plug in your unit. Make sure your power source is a grounded 120 VAC outlet. Once you've done that, turn that bad boy on. The bad boy is your unit obviously. Once you've got it on, you've got to set up the temperature. If you're using a digital controller, then set it for 350 degrees Fahrenheit. Anywhere from that temp all the way through to 450 degrees Fahrenheit is fine. Once you've done that, just let the grill do its thing for at least half an hour to an hour, at that same temp. If you're going analog with your controller, then please set the temp to high.

The Seasoning Procedure

More often than not, the initial burn in is more than enough to get rid of all the contaminants and oils and stuff, for most makes of the wood pellet smoker grill. However, there are some manufacturers which recommend you go a step further than just doing your initial burn in.

So the recommended second step to breaking in your wood pellet smoker grill is to season it. This is very simple. All you need is a pound of bacon, and you're good to go. Just cook that on your grill at a temperature of 350 degrees Fahrenheit. Set a pan on your grill grates, and then slap on the bacon. Grill for an hour, and you should have properly seasoned your grill.

These days, a lot of the wood pellet smoker grills are made of stainless steel, or aluminium reinforced steel, with a powder coat finished at a high temperature. If you're using one like this, then you don't have to worry about seasoning your grill.

Beware The Hot Spots!

When it comes to wood pellet smoker grills, there are those makes which are king, and those which could only ever hope to be king. Not unlike with every other thing under the sun which is manufactured. That said, you need to learn all you can about your grill, so you can consistently make only the most tender, juiciest, moistest, most delicious grills and barbecues which your family and friends will be unable to stop raving about! To master the wood pellet smoker grill, you must **know** the wood pellet smoker grill. That's some Yoda for you right there. All you need to master it is a few practice sessions, and you're good.

First things first, you've got to test out the surface temperatures of your grill, so you can check to be sure where you've got uniform heat, and where the hot spots are lurking. We're going to do a little something called "the biscuit test." Here's how that works: Grab some fridge biscuits, and then put them in the center, corners, front, and back of the grill. Now cook them, following the instructions written on the pack. This is how you're going to learn which parts of your unit are hot, and which parts are cooler than the others, like Mike Posner. Once you've done this, you will now know where to put your food if you want it to cook faster, or slower.

There's a fancier, more technical way to check for hot spots, if you want to be that guy. All you need is a remote temperature probe, which you will use to check the same spots as in the biscuit test method. Just make sure each of those spots has a remote temperature probe. Then you can check the temperature, comparing it to the temperature you set on your controller. If you notice any differences, then write them down, so you don't forget.

Now, I should warn you: You **will** find differences, no matter how good your controller is. It's all on account of where the RTD or thermocouple is located. All you have to do to balance out the differences is simply to adjust the controller's temperature settings, so you can get the precise amount of heat you need.

How to Clean Your Wood Pellet Smoker Grill

If you're one of those people who don't bother cleaning out stuff they should — like the toaster, the oven, or the grill or something — this is not going to fly here. You've got to keep your wood pellet smoker grill as clean as you can get it, at all times. It's not going to cost you an arm and a leg. All you need are just a few minutes each time.

If you're not sold on why you should keep your wood pellet smoker grill clean at all times, let me help you see the light. If you keep them clean, then every time you cook, the smoke that permeates your meals will be clean, and fresh. Nothing is more disgusting than stale smoke!

If you want the very best of results, then you've got to use foil on your grease drip pan. Also, be sure to always replace the foil after two to four cooking sessions, or after each long cooking session. If you insist on not using foil, then you must make sure you get all the residue which builds up on your drip pan clean out. Don't let it all accumulate until you've got a nasty looking cake there. The last thing you need is to burn off old grease which has gone rancid at higher temperatures. The fumes are nasty, and they are bad for your meals.

The correct way to clean is right after each cooking session. You want to clean while the grill gates are still nice and hot, using a wire brush specifically for barbecue to scrape it all clean. Also, wipe down the grates on both sides thoroughly, using paper towels. Don't skimp on this, ever. When you're cleaning the grates and the pit, it would be in your best interests to do this with a pair of rubber gloves — preferably the disposable kind.

As soon the pit is cool as an icy cucumber, you can then take out the drip pan and clean the ash off the firepot and the pit's body, using a shop vacuum cleaner. No matter how high end and efficient your wood pellet smoker grill is, there's going to be some ash. If you let the ash pile up, then you'll find that your wood pellet smoker grill is not as efficient as it used to be, and that the igniter rod will have problems lighting up the pellets when you start your unit up. As if that weren't bad enough, there's a huge chance the ash that's there could somehow be blown about, causing it to settle on your meat as you cook. No one signs up to eat ashy meat. You don't need that. So clean out the ash!

On The Matter of Foil

When it comes to foil, there are two schools of thought. The first would rather not use foil, preferring to simply scrape off all the residue which has been burnt on to the drip pan from past cooking sessions. The second prefer to toss out the old foil and replace it with new foil. This is what I think is the better option.

It's incredibly easy to clean, when you make use of foil, but besides that, the last thing I want is to have the residue from previous cooking sessions and old grease burnt off and ruining the smoke I'm infusing my meats with. It's much better to have a drip pan that is clean all the time, and the only way to do this is using foil. If you can see my point, and you'd like to use foil, then make sure you go for the kind that is heavy-duty. At least 18 inches wide. You can find that kind of foil roll at the big box stores.

Let's Talk Wood Pellets

Food grade barbecue wood pellets are usually cylindrical in shape. They are made up of hardwood sawdust which has been compressed. The raw materials to make them are gotten from saw mills which deal with whole logs, or from orchards. The best of wood suppliers will always oversee the entire process of manufacture, and make sure that there's no harmful foreign contaminants, or chemicals which could affect you adversely. The only additives you will find to the wood pellets are just vegetable oils. Even more awesome is the fact that they burn really clean, and after use, they do not leave much ash at all.

There are two things to barbecue wood pellets: Flavor, and wood. The wood could be alder base, or oak. The amount of each varies greatly from one manufacturer to another. There could be a 35 percent base wood, and a 65% flavor hardwood. If you're talking about flavors like maple, oak, hickory, and apple, you are more than likely to find it's 100 percent flavor hardwood, with no base wood. You can even find some wood pellets which are blends of various flavors. If you're dealing with a manufacturer who is west of the Mississippi river, then your base wood will be Alder. If they're to the west of the Mississippi, then it's going to be oak.

Storing Your Wood Pellets

The best way to store your wood pellets is to keep them some place nice and dry, like in your shed, or garage. If you've got a wooden pallet, then you can keep your pellets there. The reason you want some place nice and dry is that if you keep them anywhere else, then they are likely to get wet. Or you might find that they're being degraded by the moisture in the atmosphere, especially if you've had them for quite a while. Once this happens, they won't light up like they should, and they could ruin your auger too.

So how do you prevent this? As soon as you open up a bag of wood pellets, make sure you keep what's left of it in a charcoal or wood pellet dispenser. You can also store them in brand new trash cans, plastic buckets which have lids, a huge container for pet food, or basically any airtight container, so your wood pellets can stay nice and dry. Make sure you keep the containers in a dry shed, or in your garage.

Pairing Pellets and Proteins

In the past, our ancestors smoked meats so that they could last longer. Now, we do that just to give it some delicious flavor. You'll find that each wood has it's very own flavor which goes better with some meats than others. The pairings of smoke and meat can be anywhere from mild to strong.

Alder: This has just a hint of aroma and sweetness. It works best with poultry, lamb, pork, beef, salmon and other kinds of fish as well.

Apple: This is a very popular choice, and very strong as well. It gives smoke best described as succulent, sweet, yet mild. It works great with lamb, game, poultry, and port.

Cherry: Sometimes it gives the lighter kinds of meats a bit of a rosy color, which makes it seem like the meats haven't been thoroughly cooked, so beware of that. It has a fruity flavor that is slightly sweet. It works best with game, beef, pork, and poultry.

Hickory: Love bacon? Then you'll love hickory, as it gives your meats a flavor reminiscent of bacon. It's also one of the most popular woods used. It works great with fish, beef, pork, poultry, and game.

Maple: This one has a mildly sweet tang to it. It works great with beef, poultry, and pork.

Mesquite: You'll be able to tell when mesquite was used to smoke your meat right away. Its flavor is very unique. It's quite strong and really spicy. Tangy, too. It works great with fish and beef.

Oak: It's a touch milder than hickory, but definitely much stronger than the other fruit woods out there. Pairs well with fish and beef.

Pecan: This one has a nutty, somewhat spicy flavor. It pairs perfectly with poultry, pork, and beef.

Blends: Bends have very strong, very prominent smoky flavors. They work well with game, beef, poultry, and pork.

Chapter Two: Accessories and Tips

Before you get to the business of grilling and barbecuing, you're going to need some accessories to make things a lot easier for you to deal with. Here are a few:

A Pair of Scissors, and A Set of Knives: These are definitely indispensable. So keep them handy, or buy a new set if your old one is a bit... Meh. You need the knives because you're going to be cutting a lot of meat, whether raw or cooked. You'll also need the scissors to help you out when it comes to trimming choice cuts of your meat, among other preparations you'll be doing. One of the best knives to have would be the 14-inch slicing knife which comes with a hollow edge. This is the best for cutting up large portions of meat, when you're working with poultry, roasts, and briskets.

A Digital Meat Thermometer: Get one of these babies. It's super important, because temperature matters a lot when you're working with meats. I'm not talking about the temperature of your meat on the outside, either. I'm talking about the internal temperatures. You may have a wood pellet smoker grill which has more than a couple of probes, but you should still get yourself another one, so that you can use it to double check that everything is hunky dory.

If it so happens that your wood pellet smoker grill did not come with a meat probe, then you cannot do better than one of those barbecue thermometers which work wirelessly and remotely. Invest in a few, because there's no chance you're only grilling one piece of meat all the time. You have got to be careful whenever you're putting a thermometer into your meat, whether it's the instant-read kind, or the remote barbecue kind. Always insert the probe into the thickest portions of the meat, and make sure your probe is not in contact with bone.

A Smoker Box: With the smoker box, you could actually cold smoke a variety of things like jerky, salmon, nuts, meats, and even cheese. If you need something to store your foods in the meantime, and you need it to keep your food warm or at the proper serving temp, then you definitely could use your smoker box for this purpose as well. Go on and contact the manufacturer to check if they can fit your unit with one of these babies. You'll be glad you did!

Searing Grates: There are all sorts of searing grates. It all depends on the make and model of your wood pellet smoker grill. The best thing about searing grates is that you can use them for both direct and indirect flame tech. All you've got to do is contact your manufacturer, so they can let you know the best sort of searing grills which would go with your wood pellet smoker grill. With a searing grate, you get to grill whatever cuts of meat you've got, and you'll end up with some high quality grills, which once upon a time was the domain of the fanciest of steakhouses only.

Open Flame Tech, Flame Zone, Direct Flame: If you've got a good wood pellet smoker grill, then chances are it has the tech that allows you do your grilling and barbecuing with direct flame. In the past, it used to be that you could only do your cooking with indirect flames. However, you cannot grill whatever the heck you want to with direct flame tech, or whatever name the manufacturer of your wood pellet smoker grill has decided to call it (it's really all the same thing.) The very best makes will let you grill at temps even higher than 500 degrees Fahrenheit.

A Rib Rack: This will let you cook anywhere from four slabs to eight slabs of spare ribs at a go. The amount you can cook at any one time would depend on the surface area of your wood pellet smoker grill.

A Chicken Wing/Leg Hanger: Want to cook yourself some chicken wings, or legs? Then you're going to need these hangers. They don't cost much, and you can find them just about anywhere. Just a quick Google search should show you where you can buy it. What they do is they make it easier for the smoke to get into the meat. They also allow the heat to get around your grill as evenly as possible, so that your chicken is properly cooked. Oh, and as an added bonus, you get to have healthier chicken, since the fat drips out of it. Talk about basting with ease!

Barbecue Insulated Gloves: What I love about these gloves is that they are flexible, and really light, yet they offer all the protection I need when I'm doing what I do with really hot food as I work. To maintain these, all you have to do is wash them by hand. Please make sure the soap you use to wash them are mild. Then you rinse the gloves, hang them, and let them drip dry.

Teflon Coated Fiberglass Mats: these are useful for indirect cooking. It's the only way you can prevent your food from getting all stuck on your precious grill grates. What this means for you is that you don't get a headache on account of the mess you'd have had to clean up if you didn't use one of these. Don't worry, they are approved by the FDA, and are very safe for your dishwasher.

A Pizza Paddle: Did you know you can use your wood pellet smoker grill to make the tastiest, crispiest, most delicious pizza you'll ever have in your life? It's true~ To make it easier for you to put in and take out pizzas of all sizes from your grill, you're going to need a pizza paddle. Get one. They are rather inexpensive, so maybe even get two while you're at it.

A Meat Slicer: If you're going to slice your meat, then you'd better do it right! So you should opt for a seven incher one. This will save you the stress of having to slice your food by hand. It's 2019. The caveman era is dead and gone, so do keep up by getting one of these. You'll be glad you did.

Silicone Cooking Bands: You can use these in place of toothpicks or butcher's twine. Only 2-inches, they get the job done, and are safe for your dishwasher and your food. Also, you'll be glad to know they are resistant to heat as high as 600 degrees Fahrenheit, and you can use them over and over again. Talk about the gift that keeps on giving.

A Nonstick Grilling Tray: very useful if you're working with fish, veggies, or any other foods which are small and crumbly. You can easily clean the tray with some soap and water, and then it's ready for the next use.

A Pigtail Food Flipper: This is a food flipper made of pig tails. I'm kidding. This has a nice shaft which is tapered, with a spiral snare on the end which is pretty sharp. You use this to flip your food by simply piercing the food at the edge, and then flipping it. You can use it for whatever you want, except perhaps for fish and veggies.

A Griddle: You want to make a festival of breakfast, don't you? Then get yourself one of these! You can make whatever you need to: eggs, French toast, hash browns, bacon, pancakes, sausages, whatever. You can get it all done on your griddle at the same time!

A Liquid Flavor Injector: if you want your meats to be incredibly juicy, then you're going to need one of these, or more. You can use it to inject your meats with brines, herbs, spices, marinades, and all other delicious stuff. The result? Meat so flavorful you find your soul saying "Mama mia!" Just be careful not to go overboard, because you don't want to lose the natural flavor of the meat in all that marinade and stuff.

A Bluetooth Remote Control: Because you might want to play some music from your phone on your grill. Just kidding. With a Bluetooth remote control, not only can you monitor the settings on your wood pellet smoker grill, you can also change the settings without needing to be there to touch anything! How cool is that, aye? I'm all about this device right here, since I don't have to keep going in and out of the house to check on my meats!

A Wi-Fi Controller: No kidding. Definitely look into these. I have a set of these as well. They are perfect, because you can connect with your controller from whatever device you want — laptops, phones, Kindles, tablets, desktops, whatever! All you need is the internet, and boom. You've got control over your pit, baby. This is some next level stuff, ain't it? The great thing is that some Wi-Fi controllers do more than just control. They also give you a graph that lets you have details on each cooking session. The graph will show you what temp your meat is at, and what temp your grill is at, at all times, among other useful information.

A Grill Cover: With a grill cover, you can keep your wood pellet smoker grill safe from the weather and natural wear and tear which happens. It also keeps your smoker grill nice and dry, whenever you're not using it.

A Notepad: Why does this matter? Because you want to take notes of everything you do when you're making food. You could come up with a brilliant new recipe, and you'll want to know exactly how that happened. Or you may find a better way to cook an old recipe, and simply want to keep notes so that no matter what, you get it done the exact same way every time. Sure, over time it all becomes second nature to you, but it's actually better to write it down. You can't go wrong with that, and you get something you can pass on to your kids and your kids' kids!

Now that we've covered all the basic accessories you'll need to go grilling, let's cover a few tips and techniques which will come in handy as you cook.

About The Meat, and The Seasoning

When you want some good meat, look no further than the local butcher's shop. You'll get some great cuts of sausages, poultry, and meat, and you also have the option of choosing the cuts you prefer. You'll also find that a good butcher's shop will stock up on seasonings, rubs, and sauces, for you to make some wonderful food. Your local butcher could even help you out with seasoning your meat, if you make request for that service.

About the seasoning, you want something that is not going to so overpower your meat that you cannot taste the actual meat. Also, it matters that you find a brand which works perfectly for cooking meats low-and-slow, as well as for frying, smoking, roasting, grilling and other stuff. Don't be afraid to go on an adventure seeking out the perfect seasoning.

Resting Your Meat

You've got to rest your meat right, if you want to make sure each piece remains nice and juicy. Nothing is more annoying than making some nice, juicy meat, only to have the juice drain out or something. So you want to rest your meat, whether it's turkey, brisket, pork rinds, or whatever, so that the juices are redistributed into the meat, and it stays nice and tender. Every pitmaster worth his or her salt knows to use the poor man's Cambro. What's that, you ask?

First of all, wrap up your meat in foil, twice. Make sure it's the heavy duty kind of foil. This will help you keep the juices where they belong — in the meat. Next, take your foiled meat and put it in a towel, then place it in a cooler. Make sure it's a large towel. Finally — and this is an optional step — you could fill the cooler with towels, to make sure there's less air, and the heat does not dissipate. You can then seal the cooler. Your meats should be good for about 2 hours, or even up to 6 hours tops. How long it is good for would depend on the kind of meat you use. Be careful handling the meat, as it will be hot!

USDA Recommended Internal Temperatures

If you're going to cook meat right, then you want to stick with the USDA's recommended internal temperatures. If you want to go above the figures listed, then that's fine, but it must never be below the temps I'm about to list. To make sure you're adhering to these recommended temperatures, make sure you use a food thermometer to check.

Beef, veal, pork, and lamb (including roasts, chops, and steaks): 145 degrees Fahrenheit. 3 minutes resting period.

Poultry (including whole birds, legs, thighs, wings, beasts, stuffing, and ground poultry): 165 degrees Fahrenheit.

Shellfish and other fish: 145 degrees Fahrenheit.

Setting Up Your Direct and Indirect Grill

As I've already mentioned before, you can't do much better than the wood pellet smoker grill when it comes to indirect cooking. They are designed for that explicit purpose. When you cook indirectly, you're basically making use of the heat that's being deflected to cook your meats. The result is while the cooking is slow, it's also very even.

When you use direct cooking, however, you're using the high heat directly. Your food is ready faster, but the thing is that there won't be much in the way of smoke infusion. At least you'll get those beautiful grill marks on your meat! Because some people love direct cooking, these days there are more designs of wood pellet smoker grills which have a hybrid system of both direct and indirect cooking.

To do a direct cooking setup, you may find that you've got to take out your indirect pan and replace it with a direct one. For some units, you may have to also remove a cover plate or more, or you may need to simply slide aside the top part of a combo pan so you can have it ready for direct cooking. All you have to do is slide your cover to one side or the other to open the holds or close them. The closed holes are obviously for indirect cooking, while for direct cooking, the holes are open. You do not necessarily need searing grates, but you should consider getting them. When you choose to cook directly, searing grates will give you the best results, since they are designed to help increase the heat flow, which is needed to properly sear food.

If you're setting up for indirect cooking, all you have to do is follow the instruction manual that accompanies your unit. You'll find that it's easy for the fat to fall off because the grease pan is deliberately set up to tilt toward the grease bucket. If it were not designed this way, then the grease would simply collect in the pan, and that could cause a safety hazard by increasing the risk of flare-ups.

A Few More Notes

For each recipe, I will recommend wood pellets. However, that's not the be all and end all. Do feel free to mix and match as you please. It's not like you could choose the wrong wood pellets and have the entire meal turn into a disaster.

As for ingredients, it's perfectly fine to substitute with whatever you want. You can add stuff in, take stuff out, do whatever you prefer, really. Needless to say, if you stick to the recipe, then your results are going to be completely out of this world. That said, don't be afraid to break the rules! You could come up with some amazing things yourself!

Before you begin making anything, you've got to prep. Part of that means you should read the recipe first, before you actually begin cooking. This way, if there's something you find confusing in the recipe, you can do some research to understand it better, and you won't ruin your food because you over cooked it while you were spending time trying to suss out what I meant by something or the other. Also, some of the recipes might require that you marinate something, or let something sit. So it's best to be prepared for all of that.

Whatever recipe you're making, please start off with a nice and clean grill which is already set up for indirect cooking, unless the recipe calls for direct cooking. Also, make sure your pellet hopper is full. When the time comes, make sure you always slide your probe into the thickest part of your meat, before you put the meat on the grill. No matter what cooking time I write down, always default to the temperature.

Meaning, if the cooking time is up but the temperature specified hasn't been reached, then leave the meat on until the temperature is hit. Don't be deceived by how great the meat looks on the outside. It's the inside that counts. That's why the temperature matters more than timing.

The more you cook, the more your confidence with the wood pellet smoker grill will grow, and the more you can freestyle with temperatures and timing.

Please note that the cooking times and preheating times will vary, depending on the make and model of your grill. Always make sure you thaw your food in the fridge by dunking it in some cold water, and then changing that water out every half hour. Make sure the food is fully submerged beneath the water. Either that, or use the microwave. It should have a handy defrost setting for that purpose. Whatever you do, never let it thaw out on the counter.

Make sure that you cook food until it reaches the recommended internal temps. Use a digital thermometer, and always insert the probe thermometer into the food before cooking.

Some recipes will require that you rest the protein for a bit underneath a foil tent, before you begin to carve or serve. To tent, all you have to do is fold some aluminum foil in the middle, then make it fan open so it kind of looks like a tent, and then place it over your food loosely. The whole point behind this is to keep the food nice and hot, while the juice continues to circulate, instead of evaporating.

Always remove the silver skin on your meat, before you begin to cook it. You'll find it's a really thin, membranous case, which wraps itself around your meat. You need to get rid of it prior to cooking because if you don't, it will get really tough after you've cooked it.

So use a boning knife to get rid of it.

As you cook, you'll notice that there is a point where the temperatures simple stop rising for a bit, before they resume again. This is known as the plateau, or zone, or the stall. It's natural, so don't worry about it. It could take a matter of minutes, or as long as four whole hours, and will typically happen when the temperature hits a range of 155 degrees Fahrenheit to 170 degrees Fahrenheit.

When the plateau happens, please do not turn up the temperature. Just wait it out. If you can't wait it out, then you can use a nifty little trick known as the Texas crutch so you don't have to deal with the stall and you can speed up your cooking. All you have to do is take the meat off the heat when the internal temperature hits 160 degrees Fahrenheit, and then you use aluminum to double wrap the meat, leaving the probes you inserted before still in the meat. You should wrap the probe in foil as well. Then you can put the meat back on the grill till it hits the temperature you're going for.

Want to carve your meat like a pro? Then carve it across the grain, not along it. All you need to do to find the grain's direction is to look for where the lines run parallel in the meat. Then simply slice perpendicularly to those lines.

Please be safe as you cook. Always make sure you keep your skin protected. Remember that one little accessory I mentioned earlier? The gloves? Use them. You can get the sort that is free of latex, and is food grade. Get the nitrile kind. They are great for working with raw meat and really hot peppers.

Make sure that your prep space is spic and span. If you can, use plastic food wrap along with some heavy duty aluminum foil to cover the area, so it's easier to clean up after, and you know that your workspace is one hundred percent sanitary.

Whatever you do, never use curing salt to season your food, either as you're cooking, or about to eat. If you have too much, it could be deadly. Use it only for curing meats, and even then in small amounts.

Finally, you should know that the wood pellet smoker grill produces less smoke, the higher the temperature is. So you won't notice any smoke if the temperature is above 300 degrees Fahrenheit, for most grills. So when a recipe requires really high temperatures, then feel free to use whatever pellets you have on hand, as they won't affect the flavor of your meats at all.

Now we have finally come to the end of this chapter about accessories and the general tips you need to keep in mind when creating sumptuous dishes with your wood pellet smoker grill. I don't know about you, but I'm really excited to introduce you to some really yummy recipes! The important thing you need to keep in mind as regards all of this is you should have fun! Food should be fun, from cooking, to eating. This is my philosophy. That said, without further ado, let's jump right in!

Chapter Three: Appetizers and Sides

Are you excited? I know I am! So let's get right to it!

Smashed Potato Casserole

I cannot begin to tell you how awesome this is! If you want to make sure your friends and family never leave your home, ever, then make them this deliciously decadent smashed potato casserole. It's so amazing, and so easy to prepare. The recipe is so flavorful you just cannot resist going for seconds, thirds, and tenths! If you would like to tweak this recipe a bit, then please, go right ahead and do so. However, maybe for the first time, you should do it the way I will direct in the book, and then after that you can go nuts with it!

Serving Size: 8 adult-sized humans

Prep time: 10 - 45 mins

Cook time: 45 - 60 mins

Rest time: 10 mins

Best pellets: All

1 small red onion, thinly sliced

1 small green bell pepper, thinly sliced

1 small red bell pepper, thinly sliced

1 small yellow bell pepper, thinly sliced

3 cups mashed potatoes

8 - 10 bacon slices

¼ cup bacon grease or salted butter (½ stick)

¾ cup sour cream

1 ½ teaspoons barbecue rub

3 cups shredded sharp cheddar cheese (divided)

4 cups hash brown potatoes (frozen)

Grill Prep

1. Get that bacon cooking over medium heat in a large skillet. Cook till nice and crisp. Aim for 5 minutes on both sides. Then set aside your bacon.
2. Pour the bacon grease into a glass container and set aside.
3. Using the same skillet, warm up the butter or bacon grease over medium heat. When warm enough, sauté bell peppers and red onions. You're aiming for al dente. When done, set it all aside.
4. Grab a casserole dish, preferably one that is 9 by 11 inches. Spray with some nonstick cooking spray, then spread the mashed potatoes out, covering the entire bottom of the dish.
5. Add the sour cream as the next layer over the potatoes. When you're done, season it with some of the barbecue rub.
6. Next, create a new layer with the sautéed veggies over the potatoes, leaving the butter or grease in the pan.
7. Sprinkle your sharp cheddar cheese — just 1½ of the cups. Then add the frozen hash brown potatoes.
8. Scoop out the rest of the bacon grease or butter from the sautéed veggies, all over the hash browns, and then top it all off with some delicious crumbled bacon bits.
9. Add the rest of the sharp cheddar cheese (1½ cups) over the whole thing, and then use some aluminum foil to cover the casserole dish.

On the Grill

1. Set up your wood pellet smoker grill for indirect cooking. Preheat that bad boy to 350 degrees Fahrenheit. Use whatever pellets you like.
2. Let the whole thing bake for 45 - 60 minutes. Ideally, you want the cheese to bubble.
3. Take it out and let it sit for about 10 minutes.
4. Serve!

A little something to keep in mind: You can use leftover mashed potatoes or instant mashed potatoes. They're both amazing! If you're watching your weight and counting your calories, then you can use extra-virgin olive oil rather than butter, reduced-fat cheese, and fat-free sour cream. Also, you can just forget about bacon, or opt for turkey bacon instead.

Atomic Buffalo Turds

These are so divine! Honestly I'm not sure you're going to want to try making anything else for a while after you've had some of these bad boys in your mouth. So what exactly is an atomic buffalo turd, and perhaps more importantly, *why the heck are we even eating anything called a buffalo turd, atomic or not?!* Fair question. Perhaps a description will help you understand the awesomeness you're looking at.

The Atomic Buffalo Turd is basically jalapeno peppers which have been stuffed with some delicious, creamy cream cheese, and then topped off with some yummy sausages, sometimes wrapped in bacon, if that's your thing. With each bite, it's like you've died and gone to Heaven.

Now I know you're probably thinking you want nothing to do with jalapenos because of how spicy they are, but you've got nothing to fear. The thing about jalapeno peppers is that the longer you cook them for, the milder they get. So you can stop worrying about getting red in the face now, or having a bad case of the hot blasts later on in the bathroom. If you're still feeling skeptical, don't worry. I've got you. You can just opt for baby bell peppers instead. But come on! Live a little! A little bit of spice is nice. Don't make me say it twice!

Serving: 6 - 10 adult-sized humans

Prep time: 30 - 45 mins

Cook time: 90 - 120 mins

Rest Time: 5 mins

Best Pellets: Blend, Hickory

Ingredients

8 ounces regular cream cheese (room temp)

10 jalapeno peppers (medium)

¾ cup cheddar cheese blend and shredded Monterey Jack (not necessary)

1 teaspoon smoked paprika

1 teaspoon garlic powder

½ teaspoon red pepper flakes (not necessary)

Lit'l Smokies sausages (20)

10 bacon strips, thinly sliced and halved

Grill Prep

1. Wear your food service gloves. Get your beautiful jalapenos and wash them, then slice them up along the length. Get a spoon, or a paring knife if you prefer, and use that to take out the seeds and the veins as carefully as you can, so they don't get into your eyes. Toss them. Then place the scooped out jalapenos on a veggie grilling tray, and put it all aside.
2. Get a small bowl, and mix the shredded cheese (if you're using it), the cream cheese, paprika, cayenne pepper, garlic powder, and red pepper flakes. Mix them thoroughly.
3. Next, get your jalapenos which you've hollowed out, and then stuff them with the cream cheese mix.

4. Get your Lit'l Smokies sausage, and then put it right onto each of the cheese stuffed jalapenos.
5. Grab some of the thinly sliced and halved bacon strips, and wrap them around each of the stuffed jalapenos and their sausage.
6. Grab some toothpicks. Use them to keep the bacon nicely secured to the sausage. Whatever you do, do not pierce the pepper.

On The Grill

1. Set up your wood pellet smoker grill so it's ready for indirect cooking. Get it preheated to 250 degrees Fahrenheit. Use hickory or blends for your wooden pellets.
2. Put your jalapeno peppers in and smoke them at 250 degrees Fahrenheit for anywhere from 90 minutes to 120 minutes. You want to keep it going until the bacon is nice and crispy.
3. Take out the atomic buffalo turds, and then let them rest for about 5 minutes.
4. Serve those bad boys up as delicious hors d'oeuvres!

A little something to keep in mind: You want to wear food service gloves, of the late free, nitrile kind. Especially when you're handling the jalapenos. If you use your bare hands, then you might touch your eyes or something, and then it's game over!

Brisket Baked Beans

Have you ever had really good brisket baked beans? Well, I don't care. Because you're about the make the best you've ever had! So say goodbye to Chef Bob at your favorite restaurant, because you're going to be a pro at making this bad boy at home. If you've got some leftover beef briskets, you can use them in this recipe! You'll find beans to be a great accompaniment to most meals. Beans can be your main dish, or your side dish.

Either way, it doesn't mind, and neither will you! It's incredibly easy to create, and you'll just find yourself in absolute love with the rich sweetness of it all. Your family and friends will not be able to stop eating until the last spicy spoonful of beans is gone!

Serving: 10 - 12 adult-sized humans

Prep time: 20 mins

Cook time: 90 mins - 120 mins

Rest time: 15 mins

Best pellets: All

Ingredients

1 green bell pepper (medium, diced)

1 red bell pepper (medium, diced)

1 yellow onion (large, diced)

2 - 6 jalapeno peppers (diced)

2 tablespoons olive oil (extra-virgin)

3 cups brisket flat (chopped)

1 can baked beans (28 ounces)

1 can red kidney beans (1 4ounces, rinsed, drained)

1 cup barbecue sauce

½ cup brown sugar (packed)

2 teaspoons mustard (ground)

3 cloves of garlic (chopped)

1 ½ teaspoon black pepper

1 ½ teaspoon kosher salt

Grill Prep

1. Put a skillet on the fire, on medium heat. Warm up your olive oil. Toss in the diced jalapenos, peppers, and onions. Now you're going to cook that colorful goodness until the onions become translucent. That should take about 8 minutes, or 10 minutes, tops. Stir every now and then.
2. Grab a 4-quart casserole dish. Now, in your dish, mix in the pork and beans, kidney beans, baked beans, chopped brisket, cooked peppers and onions, brown sugar, barbecue sauce, garlic, mustard, salt, and black pepper.

On The Grill

1. Set up your wood pellet smoker grill so it's ready for indirect cooking.
2. Preheat your grill to 325 degrees Fahrenheit, using whatever pellets you want.
3. Cook your brisket beans on the grill, for 90 minutes to 120 minutes. Keep it uncovered as you cook. When it's ready, you'll know, because the beans will get thicker and will have bubbles as well.
4. Rest the food for 15 minutes, before you finally move on to step number 5.
5. Serve and enjoy!

A little something to keep in mind: You can change things up by adding some more jalapeno peppers, and leaving the seeds in. It doesn't matter what pellets you choose, as at a temperature of 325 degrees Fahrenheit, there is not going to be much smoke, if any at all. If you want your beans to have a bit of smokiness to them, then you can smoke them for 30 minutes to an hour at 180 degrees Fahrenheit, before you bake them.

Twice-Baked Spaghetti Squash

You'll never get a side dish more versatile than the spaghetti squash, folks. One of the things I love about this meal is that it's really low in carbs, so you don't have to worry about no longer being able to fit into your jeans. It's the best alternative to pasta, which is super gooey. You're going to find it just as delicious as sweet potatoes or twice-baked potatoes.

Serving: 2 adult-sized humans

Prep time: 15 mins

Cook time: 45 - 60 mins

Best pellets: All

Ingredients

1 spaghetti squash (medium)

1 tablespoon olive oil (extra virgin)

1 teaspoon salt

½ teaspoon pepper

½ cup Parmesan cheese (grated, divided)

½ cup mozzarella cheese (shredded, divided)

Grill Prep

1. As carefully as you can, cut the squash along the length in half. Make sure you're using a knife that's large enough, and sharp enough. Once you're done, take out the pulp and the seeds from each half with a spoon.
2. Rub the insides of each half of the squash with some olive oil. When you're done with that, sprinkle the salt and pepper.

On The Grill

1. Set up your wood pellet smoker grill for indirect cooking.
2. Preheat your grill to 375 degrees Fahrenheit with your preferred wood pellets.
3. Put each half of the squash on the grill. Make sure they're both facing upwards on the grill grates, which should be nice and hot.
4. Bake for 45 minutes, keeping it on the grill until the internal temperature of the squash hits 170 degrees Fahrenheit. You'll know you're done when you find it easy to pierce the squash with a fork.
5. Move the squash to your cutting board. Let it sit there for 10 minutes, so it can cool a bit.
6. Now, turn up the temp on your wood pellet smoker grill to 425 degrees Fahrenheit.
7. Use a fork to remove the flesh from the squash in strands by raking it back and forth. Do be careful, because you want the shells to remain intact. The strands you rake off should look like spaghetti, if you're doing it right.
8. Put the spaghetti squash strands in a large bowl, and then add in half of your mozzarella and half of your Parmesan cheeses. Combine them by stirring.
9. Now take that mix, and stuff it into the squash shells. When you're done, sprinkle them with the rest of the Parmesan and mozzarella cheeses.
10. Optional: You can top these with some bacon bits, if you like.
11. Allow the stuffed spaghetti squash shells you've now stuffed to bake at 435 degrees Fahrenheit for 15 minutes, or however long it takes the cheese to go brown.
12. Serve, and enjoy!

Bacon-Wrapped Asparagus

Oh sweet asparagus! How do I love thee? Let me count the ways. Sautéed, deep-fried, steamed, baked, broiled, whatever! Asparagus is simply amazing. Case closed. Now if you take something just as amazing as bacon and pair that with asparagus, what have you got? A lot of deliciousness in your mouth! There's nothing quite like bacon-wrapped asparagus, nicely grilled. Let's get into it!

Serving: 4 - 6 adult sized humans

Prep time: 15 mins

Cook time: 25 - 30 mins

Best pellets: All

Ingredients

15 - 20 spears of fresh asparagus (1 pound)

Olive oil (extra virgin)

5 slices bacon (thinly sliced)

1 teaspoon salt and pepper (or your preferred rub)

Grill Prep

1. Break off the ends of the asparagus, then trim it all so they're down to the same length.
2. Separate the asparagus into bundles — 3 spears per bundle. Then spritz them with some olive oil.
3. Use a piece of bacon to wrap up each bundle. When you're done, lightly dust the wrapped bundle with some salt and pepper to taste, or your preferred rub.

On The Grill

1. Set up your wood pellet smoker grill so that it's ready for indirect cooking.
2. Put some fiberglass mats on your grates. Make sure they're the fiberglass kind. This will keep your asparagus from getting stuck on your grill gates.
3. Preheat your grill to 400 degrees Fahrenheit, with whatever pellets you prefer. You can do this as you prep your asparagus.
4. Grill the wraps for 25 minutes to 30 minutes, tops. The goal is to get your asparagus looking nice and tender, and the bacon deliciously crispy.

Garlic Parmesan Wedges

Baked garlic Parmesan wedges are an absolutely smash heat! They are just the best, whether you're looking for a side dish, an appetizer, or a simple snack. They're super tender on the inside, yet incredibly crispy on the outside, making for one very delectable meal! If you're craving some French fries, give these a go instead! You'll have no regrets. I promise.

Serving: 3 adult sized humans

Prep time: 15 mins

Cook time: 30 - 35 mins

Best pellets: All

Ingredients

3 russet potatoes (large)

2 teaspoons of garlic powder

¾ teaspoon black pepper

1 ½ teaspoons of salt

¾ cup Parmesan cheese (grated)

3 tablespoons fresh cilantro (chopped, optional. You can replace this with flat-leaf parsley).

½ cup blue cheese (per serving, as optional dip. Can be replaced with ranch dressing).

Grill Prep

1. Use some cold water to scrub your potatoes as gently as you can with a veggie brush. When done, let them dry.
2. Slice your potatoes along the length in half. Cut each half into a third.
3. Get all the extra moisture off your potato by wiping it all away with a paper towel. If you don't do this, then you're not going to have crispy wedges!
4. In a large bowl, throw in your potato wedges, some olive oil, garlic powder, salt, garlic, and pepper, and then toss them with your hands, lightly. You want to make sure the spices and oil get on every last wedge.
5. Neatly place your wedges on a nonstick grilling tray, or pan, or basked. The single layer kind. Make sure it's at least 15 x 12 inches.

On The Grill

1. Set up your wood pellet smoker grill so it's ready for indirect cooking.
2. Preheat your grill to 425 degrees Fahrenheit, with whatever wood pellets you like.
3. Set the grilling tray upon your preheated grill. Roast the wedges for 15 minutes before you flip them. Once you turn them, roast them for another 15 minutes, or 20 tops. The goal is to get your potatoes as tender as you can. You'll know you've got it right when you can insert a fork easily into the potato. The outside should be a nice, crispy, golden brown.
4. Sprinkle your wedges generously with the Parmesan cheese. When you're done, garnish it with some parsley, or cilantro, if you like. Serve these bad boys up with some ranch dressing, or some blue cheese, or just eat them that way!

Roasted Veggies

Whatever your main dish is, veggies are the best way to complement it. Just imagine these yummy, caramelized, crispy, hot, and fresh veggies in your mouth, nicely flavored with herbs, garlic oil, and good ol' olive oil! I guarantee you'll want some of this.

Serving: 4 adult sized humans

Prep time: 20 mins

Cook time: 20 - 40 mins

Best pellets: All

Ingredients

1 cup mushrooms (small, halved)

1 cup cauliflower florets

1 yellow squash (medium, sliced, halved)

I zucchini (medium, sliced, halved)

1 red bell pepper (medium, chopped into 2-inch bits)

1 red onion (small, chopped into 2-inch bits)

6 asparagus spears (medium stemmed, cut into 1-inch bits)

6 ounces carrots (small baby carrots)

¼ cup olive oil (roasted, garlic-flavored, extra-virgin)

2 tablespoons balsamic vinegar

3 garlic cloves (minced)

1 teaspoon thyme (dried)

1 teaspoon oregano (dried)

½ teaspoon black pepper

1 teaspoon garlic salt

Grill Prep

1. Grab a large bowl. Put the mushrooms, cauliflower florets, zucchini, red bell pepper, yellow squash, red onions, asparagus, carrots, and tomatoes in it.
2. Splash in some olive oil. Then add in your garlic, thyme, oregano, black pepper, garlic salt, and balsamic vinegar.
3. Toss, toss, toss! You want to make sure all the veggies get some love from the oil, spices, and herbs.
4. As evenly as you can, scatter about the spiced veggies on your nonstick grilling basket, or tray, or pan. Best if the size is 15 x 12 inches.

On The Grill

1. Set up your wood pellet smoker grill so it's all ready for indirect cooking.
2. Preheat your grill to 425 degrees Fahrenheit with whatever wood pellets you please.
3. Move the grilling tray loaded with veggies to your preheated grill. Now roast those delicious veggies for 20 to 40 minutes. You want them to be al dente. As soon as they are, take them off the grill and serve them!

Hickory Smoked Moink Ball Skewers

You haven't lived if you haven't had some of these delicious hickory smoked moink ball skewers! Usually, you'll find moink balls can be bought from the store, and are typically thawed, wrapped up in yummy bacon which is held in place with toothpicks. If you're wondering what the heck a moink ball is, you're about to find out! "Moink" is basically a combination of the words "moo" and "oink," so that should give you a clue what's in it. That said, this ain't your average moink ball. You're going to love this one, becomes it's got a little extra oomph to it.

Serving: 6 to 9 adult sized human (each one gets 2 -3 balls!)

Prep time: 30 mins

Cook time: 60 - 75 mins

Best pellets: Hickory

Ingredients

½ pound pork sausage (ground)

½ pound ground beef (80% lean)

1 egg (large)

½ cup red onions (minced)

½ cup Parmesan cheese (grated)

½ cup Italian bread crumbs

¼ cup parsley (finely chopped)

¼ cup milk (whole)

2 garlic cloves (minced) or 1 teaspoon garlic (crushed)

1 teaspoon oregano

½ teaspoon kosher salt

½ teaspoon black pepper

¼ cup barbecue sauce

½ pound bacon slices (thinly sliced, halved)

Grill Prep

1. Mix up the ground pork sausage, ground beef, bread crumbs, onion, egg, parsley, Parmesan cheese, garlic, milk, oregano, salt, and pepper in a large bowl. Whatever you do, don't overwork your meat.
2. Make meatballs of 1½ ounces each. They should be about 1½ in width. Put them on your Teflon-coated fiberglass mat.
3. Wrap up each meatball in half a slice of your thinly sliced bacon.
4. Spear your moink balls, three to a skewer.

On The Grill

1. Set up your wood pellet smoker grill so that it's nice and ready for indirect cooking.
2. Preheat your grill to 225 degrees Fahrenheit, with your hickory wood pellets.
3. Smoke the skewered moink balls for half an hour.
4. Turn up the temperature to 350 degrees Fahrenheit, and keep it that way until the internal temperature of your skewered moink balls hits 175 degrees Fahrenheit, which should take about 40 to 45 minutes, max. What you're going for is crispy bacon.

5. When the bacon gets nice and crispy, brush your moink balls with whatever barbecue sauce you like. Ideally, you should do this in the last five minutes of your cook time.
6. Serve the moink ball skewers while they're hot!

A little something to keep in mind: For a burst of flavor and more moisture, use ground beef that has 20% fat at least.

Chapter Four: Brines and Rubs

We're going to get started with brines and rubs in this chapter. If we're talking about flavor, then there's no way you could possibly have any without brines and rubs. They're what make it all worthwhile, so let's get into it!

Pork Brine

You'll find that pork brine is the perfect option when it comes to grilling, baking, smoking, and roasting. With pork brine, you have all the moisture you need in your meats, and you'll find that your meal will be bursting with flavor and extreme succulence with each bite. Most chefs are hesitant to share their brining methods, but for good reason.

Here are a few ingredients you could add to your own version of pork brine, so you can come up with your own unique blend. Now, remember, none of these are absolutes. You can feel free to mix and match as you please! Experiment, and you could come up with something that makes you a million dollars, and a million happy taste buds.

Amount: 1 gallon

Prep time: 15 minutes

Ingredients

1 gallon water (filtered)

¾ cup brown sugar

¾ cup kosher salt

1 cup 100% apple juice (optional, if you need to upgrade the flavor)

2 garlic cloves (smashed)

2 sprigs of thyme (or rosemary, if you prefer)

1 tablespoon mustard powder

⅛ teaspoon red pepper flakes

½ teaspoon black peppercorns

How to Make It

1. Grab a brining container, or a sealable plastic bag, and put all the ingredients in it.
2. Mix it all up until it's nicely blended
3. Make sure your meat is completely covered by the mixture
4. Keep it in your fridge.

Pork Brine Guide

For whole pork loin, make it 2 to 4 days. For pork chops about 1 to 1 ½ inches thick, make it half a day to a whole day. Whole pork tenderloin only needs anywhere from 6 hours to 12 hours.

Poultry Brine

Poultry brine is the best if you need some flavor and moisture in your poultry and chicken meals. Also the best for smoking, grilling, roasting, and baking. As usual, you can mix and match as needed, so you can get a taste that is uniquely yours. You could try adding in some soy sauce, garlic, oregano, Italian dressing, rosemary, and/or lemon, if you want to. Feel free to play with this stuff!

Amount: 1 gallon

Prep time: 15 mins

Ingredients

1 gallon water (filtered)

½ cup salt (kosher or pickling)

½ cup white sugar

Lemon (fresh, sliced, halved, quartered, or grated zest)

2 bay leaves

½ cup olive oil

½ cup Italian salad dressing

¾ cup soy sauce

2 - 4 garlic cloves (smashed)

Fresh and/or fried spices and herbs (parsley, oregano, sage, cloves, thyme, rosemary, etc.)

How to Make

1. Grab a brining container, or a sealable plastic baggie, and put all your ingredients in.
2. Mix it all up until nicely blended
3. Make sure the brine generously covers your meat.
4. Keep it in the fridge.

Poultry Brine Guide

Working with about 4 to 5 pounds of chicken? Then you'll need 4 to 12 hours. Chicken pieces will need 1 to 2 hours. Chicken breasts need 1 hour. Turkey breasts need 5 to 8 hours. Whole turkey takes 1 to 2 days. A Cornish game hen needs 1 to 2 hours.

Trout and Salmon Brine

Amount: 5 to 6 cups.

Prep time: 15 mins

Ingredients

5 cups water (filtered, for trout)

4 cups water (filtered, for salmon)

1 cup soy sauce (or teriyaki sauce)

½ cup salt (pickling or kosher)

½ cup brown sugar

2 tablespoons onion powder

2 tablespoons garlic powder

1 tablespoon cayenne pepper (optional)

How to Make

1. Grab a sealable bag (the 1-gallon kind) or a 2-gallon plastic bag (make sure it's food grade). Put all your ingredients in.
2. Keep in your fridge.

Rubs

Ultra-Dry Rub

This is perfect for poultry, but can work just as well with pork. You can try this dry rub on tri-tip roasts. I bet you're going to love them! All you need are 14 ingredients to make this rub.

Amount: 3 cups

Prep time: 25 mins

Ingredients

¼ cup seasoned salt

¼ cup garlic salt

1 ¼ cups sugar

¼ cup and an added 1 ½ teaspoons celery salt

½ cup paprika

¼ cup onion salt

2 tablespoons black pepper

3 tablespoons chili powder

1 tablespoon lemon pepper

2 teaspoons ground sage (dried)

2 teaspoons celery seed

1 teaspoon mustard (dried)

½ teaspoon cayenne pepper

½ teaspoon ground thyme

How to Make

1. Grab all your ingredients, pour them into a medium bowl, and mix it all up until it's perfectly blended.
2. Keep somewhere cool, away from all light. You want to store this in an airtight sealable bag or jar.

Cajun Spice Rub

This is great for all pork, seafood, and poultry.

Amount: ⅓ cup

Prep time: 15 mins

Ingredients

2 teaspoons garlic powder

1 tablespoon salt (kosher)

1 teaspoon black pepper

2 teaspoons paprika

1 teaspoon oregano

½ teaspoon cayenne pepper

1 teaspoon thyme

½ teaspoon red pepper flakes (not necessary)

For chicken, add the following additional ingredients:

½ teaspoon rosemary

½ teaspoon sage

How to Make It

1. Grab a little bowl, put in all the ingredients, and mix until all ingredients have blended properly.
2. Store in a sealable plastic bag or an airtight jar away from all light, in a cool and dry place.

Seafood Seasoning

If you want your seafood to have a lot of oomph, then you definitely cannot do without some seasoning! Whether it's crab, oysters, shrimp, whatever, seafood seasoning is what makes your seafood meals and smokes stand out. You can also use these on salads too. How neat is that? All you have to do is play with the ingredients and the amounts, to make this all your own.

Amount: 1 cup

Prep time: 20 mins

Ingredients

1 tablespoon celery salt

2 tablespoons onion powder

2 tablespoons mustard (dried)

2 teaspoons black pepper

1 tablespoon paprika (smoked)

½ teaspoon allspice (ground)

½ teaspoon cloves (ground)

1 teaspoon cayenne pepper

¼ teaspoon ginger (ground)

⅛ teaspoon cinnamon (ground)

How to Make It

1. In a small bowl, mix all your ingredients, until they are nicely blended.
2. Store them in a cool, dry place, using a sealable plastic baggie, or an airtight jar, keeping it away from all light.

Poultry Seasoning

Sure, you could go to the store and buy yourself some poultry seasoning, but rather than do that, you should get your own spices and herbs, and make your very own special combination. You'll be glad you took the time out to do this. It doesn't get better than homemade, baby.

Amount: ¼ cup

Prep time: 15 mins

Ingredients

1 teaspoon rosemary leaves

1 teaspoon marjoram (ground)

1 teaspoon thyme (ground)

1 teaspoon sage (ground)

½ teaspoon paprika (smoked)

1 teaspoon celery salt

½ teaspoon nutmeg (ground)

¼ teaspoon black pepper

½ teaspoon paprika (smoked)

½ teaspoon onion powder

How to Make It

1. Mix all the ingredients in a little bowl, until it's all blended properly.
2. Keep in a cool, dry, and dark place, using an airtight container, or a sealable plastic baggie.

Chapter Five: Poultry

Ah, poultry. Isn't it amazing? So delicious, when done right. In this chapter, I'll be giving you some of the most amazing poultry recipes ever. Let's dig in!

Grilled Quarters

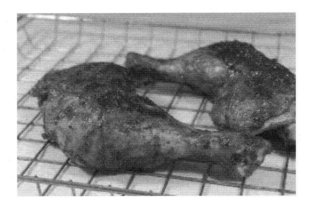

What's not to love about grilled chicken quarters? They are so easy to make, easy on your pocket, incredibly moist, and ever so meaty. If you love you some dark meat, then you're going to love grilled quarters. For a lot of recipes, you've got to have the meat hit 165 degrees Fahrenheit. However, this rule only applies to white meat from chicken. You can hit temperatures as high as 180 degrees Fahrenheit if you want to. You'll learn that dark meat is an exception to that rule, and it will remain ever so moist and divine in your mouth at temperatures beyond 180 degrees Fahrenheit.

Serving: 4 adult sized humans

Prep time: 20 mins (add in an extra 120 mins to 240 mins for marinating)

Cook time: 60 - 90 mins

Rest time: 15 mins

Best pellets: All

Ingredients

4 chicken quarters (fresh or thawed)

4 - 6 tablespoons olive oil (extra-virgin)

4 tablespoons ultra-dry rub

Grill Prep

1. Get rid of any excess fat and skin by trimming them off.
2. Peel the chicken skin back as carefully as you can, and then rub some olive oil under it, and then on it.
3. Grab your seasoning, and season your chicken beneath the skin, on top of it, and on the back of it with the ultra-dry rub.
4. Wrap up your seasoned chicken quarters properly in a plastic wrap. Keep it in the fridge for 120 to 240 minutes, so that the flavors can really get into the meat.

On The Grill

1. Set up your wood pellet smoker grill so it's ready for indirect cooking.
2. Preheat your grill to 325 degrees Fahrenheit, with whatever pellets your heart desires.
3. Put the chicken on your grill. Cook for an hour at 325 degrees Fahrenheit.
4. When the hour is up, turn up the temperature to 400 degrees Fahrenheit, so your chicken can be done, and the skins can be wonderfully crisp.
5. Take out the crisp chick from the grill, as soon as the internal temperature hits 180 degrees Fahrenheit, and the juices from your chicken are nice and clear. Remember, the probe should be inserted into thickest part of your chicken for accurate temperature measurement.
6. Tent your grilled chicken quarters using loose foil, for about 15 minutes.
7. Serve, and enjoy!

A little something to keep in mind: Your chicken will lose a bit of its crispiness as you tent it. This is normal.

Cajun Spatchcock Chicken

Looking for a quick way to make some delicious, roasted, smoked, juicy whole chicken without compromising on taste? Then you want to spatchcock your chicken! What the heck does that mean, you ask? Well, it's also called butterflying. It's basically taking out the backbone of the poultry, so you can press it and make it as flat as possible.

Serving: 4 adult sized humans

Prep time: 30 mins (include 90 mins for marinating)

Cook time: 150 mins

Rest time: 15 mins

Best pellets: blend, pecan, hickory

Ingredients

4 - 5 pounds chicken (young, fresh, or thawed)

4 - 6 tablespoons olive oil (extra virgin)

4 tablespoons Cajun spice rub

Grill Prep

1. Grab a cutting board and place your chicken on it face down.
2. Grab a pair of poultry o kitchen shears, and then cut along the sides of the bird's backbone to take it out.
3. Now, turn your chicken over. Then press down on it as firmly as you can, so that the breasts are flattened.
4. As carefully as possible, loosen up the thigh, breast, and drumstick skin. Peel it all back.
5. Rub a generous amount of olive oil under the skin, and on it as well.
6. Rub a generous amount of the Cajun spice rub on and under the skin, too.
7. Wrap up you're chicken in some plastic, and then let it chill out a bit in the fridge for about 3 hours, so the chicken and the spices can, you know, get to know each other on a deeper level.

On The Grill

1. Set your grill up so it's ready for indirect cooking.
2. Preheat your grill to 225 degrees Fahrenheit, using either pecan or hickory wood pellets, or a blend of your choice.
3. Insert the meat temperature probe you've got into the thickest part of the chicken, at the breast.
4. Now smoke that bad boy for 150 minutes.
5. Once that time has elapsed, crank up the heat to 375 degrees Fahrenheit, and then let it roast until the temperature probe reads 170 degrees Fahrenheit, and the thighs are 180 degrees Fahrenheit at the very least.
6. Let your chicken hang out again, this time beneath a foil tent, for just 15 minutes.
7. Once the resting time is over, carve that baby up, serve, and enjoy!

Teriyaki Smoked Drumsticks

You're going to start a riot with these bad boys! They are so vibrant in color, rich in flavor, moist, succulent, and so darn delicious! The best thing of all is that it's easy to make. If you love you some dark meat, then this is for you as well!

Serving: 4 adult sized humans

Prep time: 15 mins (include time to marinate overnight)

Cook time: 90 mins - 120 mins

Rest time: 15 mins

Best pellets: Maple, hickory

Ingredients

3 cups Teriyaki marinade and cooking sauce

3 teaspoons poultry seasoning

1 teaspoon garlic powder

10 chicken drumsticks

Grill Prep

1. Grab a medium sized bowl, mix up the cooking sauce and marinade with the garlic powder and poultry seasoning.
2. Carefully peel the skin of the drumsticks back, to make it easier for the marinade to get in there and do what it does.
3. Put the drumsticks in a 1-gallon plastic sealable baggie, or a marinating pan if you've got one of those. Pour the marinade over the drumsticks. Make sure it covers every drumstick. Keep it in your fridge overnight.
4. In the morning, turn the drumsticks over.

On The Grill

1. Set up your wood pellet smoker grill so it's ready for indirect cooking.
2. Put the skin back over the drumsticks, and then hang your drumsticks on a poultry rack for legs and wings, so they can drain onto your cooking sheet, which should be laid out on your counter as the grill preheats. Don't own a rack? Simply grab some paper towels, and pat the drumsticks dry.
3. Preheat your wood pellet smoker grill to 180 degrees Fahrenheit, with some pale or hickory wood pellets.
4. Smoke your drumsticks for 60 minutes.
5. Once the time elapses, turn up the heat to 350 degrees Fahrenheit, and then let the drumsticks cook for an extra 30 minutes to 45 minutes. You want the internal temperature of your drumsticks to hit 180 degrees Fahrenheit.
6. Tent your chicken, letting it rest for 15 minutes.
7. Serve, and enjoy!

A little something to keep in mind: Your chicken drumstick falls under the very dark meat category. As such, you will find it most forgiving. It will still hold on to moisture even when its internal temperature is at 180 degrees Fahrenheit. As a rule of thumb and a matter of caution, always choose to go higher in temperature, so you don't wind up with meat that is undercooked.

Roasted Tuscan Thighs

It really doesn't get more flavorful than chicken thighs. The meat is exceptionally succulent! One of the neat things about chicken thighs is that they are not expensive at all. If you want the best results making this recipe, then I recommend as you roast or smoke the meat, you go bone-in, with the skin on. This way, your meat will retain all the moisture to make your mouth water. If you want crispy skin as you grill this on your wood pellet smoker grill, then you've got to roast it at 350 degrees Fahrenheit, or even higher, as you cook.

Serving: 4 adult sized humans

Prep time: 20 mins (include 60 - 120 mins for marinating)

Cook time: 40 - 60 mins

Rest time: 15 mins

Best pellets: All

Ingredients

8 Chicken thighs (bone in, skin on)

3 teaspoons Tuscan seasoning

3 tablespoons olive oil (roasted, garlic-flavored, extra-virgin)

Grill Prep

1. First things first, trim off all the excess skin from your thighs. No, not your thighs. Your chicken thighs. Make sure you leave ¼ inches, so you account for the inevitable shrinkage.
2. As carefully as you can, peel the skin back, and get rid of the major fat deposits beneath the skin, and on the thigh at the back.
3. Rub some olive oil on the skin, and beneath it, as well as behind the thighs.
4. Rub the seasoning on the skin and beneath it, as well as behind the thighs.
5. Wrap up your chicken thighs in some plastic wrap, then keep it in the fridge for an hour or two, so that the flavors can really get into the meat.

On The Grill

1. Set up your grill so it's ready for indirect cooking.
2. Preheat your grill to 375 degrees Fahrenheit, with whatever pellets you like.
3. Roast your chicken thighs for 40 to 60 minutes. The time will depend on the wood pellet smoker grill you've got. You want the internal temperature to hit 180 degrees Fahrenheit.
4. Once done, rest your chicken beneath a loose foil tent for 15 minutes.
5. Serve and enjoy!

A little something to keep in mind: You'll find chicken thighs are a lot more forgiving than most meats. They'll hold on to moisture, even if you hit internal temperatures higher than 180 degrees Fahrenheit. You might find you quite like the flavor of cherry wood pellets. They'll give a nice, mildly sweet flavor to your poultry, but do keep in mind that the cherry wood pellets might cause your food to be colored red in parts, so it looks like your meat is not thoroughly cooked.

Hickory Smoked Spatchcock Turkey

This is a crowd pleaser that never fails, ever! You're going to love the combination of moist and crisp textures in your mouth. When you opt to spatchcock your turkey, you'll find that it cooks much faster, and much more evenly than your run of the mill roasted turkey.

Serving: 8 - 10 adult sized humans

Prep time: 20 mins

Cook time: 210 - 255 mins

Rest time: 20 mins

Best pellets: hickory

Ingredients

1 14-pound turkey (young, fresh or thawed)

¼ cup olive oil (roasted, garlic flavored, extra-virgin)

6 tablespoons ultra-dry rub or poultry seasoning

Grill Prep

1. Using kitchen or poultry shears, or a butcher's knife, carefully take out the turkey's backbone. Al you have to do is cut along each side of the backbone.
2. Once you're done, flatten out your spatchcocked turkey. Just press down on the breast bone, and you're good.
3. Get rid of all the unneeded fat and skin by trimming it off
4. As carefully as you can, part the skin from the breast, while leaving the skin in one piece.
5. Apply the olive oil in the cavity of the breast, beneath the skin, and on the skin itself as well.
6. Season the skin, beneath and over, as well as the breast cavity, with your seasoning or dry rub.

On The Grill

1. Set up your wood pellet smoker grill for indirect cooking.
2. Preheat your wood pellet smoker grill to 225 degrees Fahrenheit, with hickory pellets.
3. Grab your Teflon-coated fiberglass non-stick grill mat, and then place your spatchcocked turkey on it, with the skin down.
4. Smoke your turkey at a temperature of 225 degrees Fahrenheit for at least 2 hours.
5. Once the 2 hour period is up, turn up the temperature to 350 degrees Fahrenheit.
6. Keep roasting the turkey until it hits 170 degrees Fahrenheit, internally, and the juices are running nice and clear.
7. Rest your turkey under a tent for 20 minutes.
8. Carve it up, serve, then chow it down!

A little something to keep in mind: If you haven't already got one, do invest in a digital instant-read thermometer, so that you can be doubly sure the internal temperature of your turkey is just right. No one likes undercooked turkey, and it can be incredibly dangerous!

Smoked Bone-in Turkey Breast

There's no rule saying you've got to wait till some holiday or the other to enjoy some good turkey, so why not try some of this on for size? It's amazing! As a bonus, you could use it for other dishes like casseroles and sandwiches.

Serving: 6 - 8 adult sized humans

Prep time: 20 mins

Cook time: 210 - 255 mins

Rest time: 20 mins

Best pellets: pecan, hickory

Ingredients

8 - 10 pounds bone-in turkey breast

6 tablespoons olive oil (extra-virgin)

5 tablespoons ultra-dry rub or poultry seasoning

Grill Prep

1. Get rid of all the excess skin and fat from your turkey breast.
2. Part the skin from the breast, while leaving the skin whole.
3. Apply olive oil under and over the skin, and in the breast cavity as well.
4. Apply seasoning under and over the skin, as well as in the breast cavity.
5. Put your turkey breasts in a V-rack, so that it's much easier to handle. You could also choose to put it right on the grill grates, with the breast-side upwards.
6. Let the turkey breasts rest at room temp on the counter, as you preheat your wood pellet smoker grill.

On The Grill

1. Set up your wood pellet smoker grill so that it's ready for indirect cooking.
2. Preheat that bad boy to 225 degrees Fahrenheit, with your pecan or hickory pellets.
3. Smoke your turkey breasts right on the grill grates, or on your V-rack for 2 hours at 225 degrees Fahrenheit.
4. Once the 2 hours have elapsed, turn up the temperature to 325 degrees Fahrenheit, and continue roasting until your turkey hits 170 degrees Fahrenheit, and the juices run nice and clear.
5. Rest your turkey breasts beneath a loose tent of foil, for 20 minutes
6. Carve your turkey against the grain, then serve, and enjoy!

Chapter Six: Red Meat

Without further ado, let's sink our teeth into some delicious, amazing red meat recipes!

Smoked Tri-Tip Roast

If you know anything about San Joaquin Valley in California, then you know that no one there jokes with their tri-tip roast. It's only recently that this delicacy became popular in the rest of the country. This triangular cut comes off the very bottom of the sirloin primal, and is the yummiest thing you could ever have! It used to be that it was used for meat in stews, or ground up to make a hamburger. This recipe is interesting, historically speaking. There was a butcher named Bob Schutz in the 1950s who had a lot of stew meat, and a lot of hamburgers. Because of this, he chose to barbecue the meat using some red oak wood. He stumbled upon greatness!

Serving: 4 - 6 adult sized humans

Prep time: 20 mins (including overnight marinating)

Cook time: 120 mins

Rest time: 15 mins

Best pellets: blend, hickory

Ingredients

1 peeled tri-tip roast (whole, 2 ½ - 3 pounds)

3 tablespoons olive oil (roasted, garlic flavored, extra-virgin)

3 tablespoons western rub

Grill Prep

1. Rub olive oil all over the tri-tip.
2. Rub the rub all over the tri-tip.
3. Wrap your tri-tip twice with plastic, and then keep it in the fridge overnight.

On The Grill

1. Set up your wood pellet smoker grill so it's ready for indirect cooking.
2. Preheat your wood pellet smoker grill to 180 degrees Fahrenheit, with either hickory wood pellets, or a blend.
3. Stick the meat probe of your wood pellet smoker grill into your tri-tip roast, making sure you've got it in the thickest part.
4. Smoke the meat for an hour.
5. Once an hour has past, crank up the heat to 325 degrees Fahrenheit. Keep cooking until the internal temperature hits 140 degrees Fahrenheit to 145 degrees Fahrenheit.
6. Tent your smoked tri-tip, letting it rest for 15 minutes.
7. Slice your smoked tri-tip against the grain, and then serve!

A little something to keep in mind: The peeled tri-tip roasts are those that no longer have their fat cap and silver skin. Your butcher can help you with that. Also, do note that the tri-tip's grains run in various directions. Always carve along the grain as required.

Meaty Chuck Short Ribs

Beef chuck short ribs are like heaven in your mouth. They are all so tender, and so flavorful. Smoke them low and slow, and they will turn out just right. This is sure to wow your friends and family! So give it a try.

Serving: 2 - 4 adult sized

Prep time: 20 mins

Cook time: 5 - 6 hours

Rest time: 15 mins

Best pellets: hickory, mesquite

Ingredients

4-bone slab beef chuck short rubs (English cut)

3 - 4 tablespoons yellow mustard (or use extra virgin olive oil)

3 - 5 tablespoons western rub

Grill Prep

1. You need to trim off the fat cap from the ribs. Also take off the silver skin.
2. Get rid of the membrane on the bones so you can season the meat thoroughly. Just get the handle of a spoon under the membrane to lift up a piece of it. Next, grab a paper towel, and use that to hold on to the membrane, then pull it off of the bones.
3. Generously rub olive oil on your short rib slab. Get every bit of it.
4. Season every bit of your short rib slab.

On The Grill

1. Set up your wood pellet smoker grill so it's ready for indirect cooking.
2. Preheat your wood pellet smoker grill to 225 degrees Fahrenheit, using hickory wood pellets or mesquite.
3. Take the meat probe, and stick it in the thickest part of your ribs.
4. Put the short ribs on your grill, with the bone side down, and then smoke the meat for 5 hours at 225 degrees Fahrenheit.
5. After the time has elapsed, if your ribs have not yet hit an internal temperature of 195 degrees Fahrenheit at the very least, then turn up the temperature of your grill to 250 degrees Fahrenheit, and let the ribs cook until the internal temperature hits 195 degrees Fahrenheit to 205 degrees Fahrenheit.
6. Let the smoked short ribs rest beneath loose foil, tenting for 15 minutes.
7. Serve it up!

A little something to keep in mind: Using yellow mustard will shockingly not make your meat taste like mustard.

Texas-Style Brisket Flat

Everyone loves brisket. That's the best cut of beef, point, blank, period. You get the brisket from steer, specifically from the lower chest or breast. It's a tough cut, so the best way to cook it is low and slow. If you're working with a brisket flat of 6 to 8 pounds, then it will take you about 5 hours and 30 minutes to get to the ideal internal temperature of 205 degrees Fahrenheit. However, there is a way to reduce the amount of time you spend cooking which is known as the "Texas crutch."

All you have to do is double-wrap your brisket as tight as you can, using heavy duty aluminum foil. This is how you bypass the plateau to tenderize your meat as quickly as possible. In addition to the Texas crutch, you can rest the brisket for 2 to 4 hours, with the cooler and the towels like we talked about before, and you will find making brisket flats to be a breeze. It's definitely worth the time! Don't let that stop you.

Servings: 8 - 10 adult sized humans

Prep time: 45 minutes (in addition to marinating overnight, which is optional)

Cook time: 5 - 6 hours

Rest time: 2 - 4 hours

Ingredients

6 ½ pound beef brisket flat

½ cup Texas style brisket rub or whatever brisket rub you like

½ cup olive oil (roasted, garlic flavored, extra-virgin)

Grill Prep

1. Get rid of the silver skin, and trim off all the fat caps you see.
2. Slather your meat with olive oil. Be generous about it.
3. Slather the rub on your meat. You want it to be completely covered, so do not skimp on this.
4. Double wrap your brisket in some plastic wrap. Then keep it in your fridge overnight, so that your rub can really get into the meat. Or!
5. Cook your meat right away, if you'd rather not marinate.

On The Grill

1. First remove the brisket from your fridge, and then slide the temperature probe of your wood pellet smoker grill into the thickest part of your brisket.
2. Set your wood pellet smoker grill so it's ready for indirect cooking.
3. Preheat your wood pellet smoker grill to 250 degrees Fahrenheit with mesquite or oak wood pellets.
4. Smoke your brisket flat at 250 degrees Fahrenheit. You want the internal temperature to hit 160 degrees Fahrenheit. This could take 4 hours.
5. Take the brisket off the grill, double wrap it with aluminum foil while leaving the meat probe in, and then put it back on the wood pellet smoker grill.
6. Crank up the heat to 325 degrees Fahrenheit, and let the brisket cook until the internal temperature hits 205 degrees Fahrenheit. This should take two more hours.
7. Take out your brisket. Still in its foil, wrap it up in a towel, and then set it in your cooler. Then you can pack in more towels to reduce the amount of moisture that

could escape from your brisket. Cover your cooler and let the brisket rest for 2 to 4 hours.

8. Take it out, unfoil it, slice against the grain.
9. Serve and enjoy!

A little something to keep in mind: You cannot beat the tall when you're making pork butt, turkey, brisket, or any other kind of meat that is large. So whatever you do, do not give in to the temptation to crank up the temperature when the internal temperature has stalled for hours.

Chapter Seven: Pork

Go on. Admit it. You've been waiting for this, haven't you? Finally, some good freaking pork! Well, without further ado, let's dive in!

Pork Sirloin Tip Roast Three Ways

Goodness gracious, this is pure heaven! Sirloin tip roasts work great with all sorts of seasonings, marinades, rubs, injections, and cooking methods. Honestly, the recipe for this is nothing short of amazing. One bite, and you will testify that life is good!

Serving: 4 - 6 adult sized humans

Prep time: 20 mins (include overnight marinating)

Cook time: 90 mins - 180 mins (depends on the method of cooking)

Rest time: 15 mins

Best pellets: hickory, apple

Ingredients

1 pork sirloin tip roast (1 ½ to 2 pounds)

¾ cup 100% apple juice

2 tablespoons olive oil (roasted, garlic flavored, extra-virgin)

5 tablespoons ultra-dry rub or pork dry rub

Grill Prep

1. Get your roast dry by patting it with a paper towel.
2. Gran your marinade injector, fill it up with apple juice, and inject every area possibly in your roast with apple juice.
3. Slather your roast with olive oil generously.
4. Slather your roast with the rub. Make sure you get it everywhere.
5. Using 2 silicone cooking bands , or butcher's twine, truss your roast.
6. Wrap up your roast in some plastic, and then keep it in your fridge overnight.

On The Grill

1. Take out the roast from your fridge, and then set it on your counter to rest as you preheat your wood pellet smoker grill.
2. Set up your wood pellet smoker grill so it's all ready for indirect cooking.
3. Preheat your wood pellet smoker grill to 350 degrees Fahrenheit, using apple wood pellets.
4. Take off the plastic wrap, and then insert the meat probe that comes with your wood pellet smoker grill into the thickest part of your roast.
5. Roast the meat. You want it to hit an internal temperature of 145 degrees Fahrenheit. This should take you 90 minutes.
6. Tent your roast, and let it rest for 15 minutes.
7. Get rid of the cooking bands and twine, and then carve your roast, making sure you go against the grain.
8. Serve and enjoy!

Double Smoked Ham

There's a huge difference between ham cooked in the oven, and ham that has been double smoked. Double smoking as a cooking method works wonderfully well with ham, especially when you use hickory wood pellets, and you use the bone-in kind of ham.

Servings: 8 - 12 adult sized humans

Prep time: 15 mins

Cook time: 150 mins - 180 mins

Rest time: 15 mins

Best pellets: hickory, apple

Ingredients

1 boneless, cooked, ready to eat, bone-in ham (10 pounds, applewood-smoked)

Grill Prep

1. Take the ham out the package. Let it remain at room temp, for half an hour.

On The Grill

1. Set up your wood pellet smoker grill so that it's ready for indirect cooking.
2. Preheat your wood pellet smoker grill to 180 degrees Fahrenheit with whatever kind of wood was originally used for the first smoking.
3. Put the ham right on the grill grates. Smoke it at 180 degrees Fahrenheit for an hour.
4. Once an hour has elapsed, crank up the temperature to 350 degrees Fahrenheit.
5. Cook your ham until the internal temp hits 140 degrees Fahrenheit, which should be in about 90 minutes to 120 minutes.
6. Take the ham out, and then wrap it up in some foil for 15 minutes to rest.
7. Now carve against the grain. Serve, and enjoy!

A little something to keep in mind: You must notice the difference between these two kinds of hams: "ready to eat," and "ready to cook." The ready to eat ham is fully cooked, so you only need to get the internal temp up to 140 degrees Fahrenheit. The ready to cook hams, however, are cooked only partially. So you need to get them to an internal temperature of 160 degrees Fahrenheit.

Tender Grilled Loin Chops

Want to make sure that your pork loin chops are one hundred percent tender? Then you want them to be at least an inch thick! It's much better if you cut them up yourself. Also, when you brush your loin chops with that miraculous, extra-virgin olive oil, you'll find that the juices are naturally sealed in. That said, you need to be mindful, because the last thing you want to do is to overcook your chops. Too much of a good thing, and all that.

Serving: 6 adult sized humans

Prep time: 10 mins (add in the optional 12 - 24 4hours needed for brining)

Cook time: 12 - 15 mins

Rest time: 5 mins

Best pellets: All

Ingredients

6 center-cut boneless loin pork chops

2 tablespoons olive oil (roasted, garlic flavored, extra-virgin)

2 quarts pork brine

2 teaspoons black pepper

Grill Prep

1. Trim off the excess fat, as well as the silver skin from your pork chops.
2. Grab the pork chops and set them in brine, in a 1-gallon sealable baggie. Keep that in the fridge for 12 hours, or until the morning.
3. Take out the pork chops from your brine, and then get them dry by patting them with paper towels.
4. Slather all pork chops with some olive oil, getting all the sides.
5. Season all sides of your pork chops with pepper. We don't need salt, because the salt we need is all in the brine.
6. Let your pork chops settle down a bit, as the wood pellet smoker grill heats up.

On The Grill

1. Set up your wood pellet smoker grill so that you're good to go with direct cooking. For this, you will need your searing grates. Spray your searing grates with some cooking spray.
2. Set your grill to high, or simply preheat your grill to 50 degrees Fahrenheit, making use of whatever pellets you want.
3. Sear your pork chops on one side, for just three minutes
4. Flip your pork chops around by 90 degrees, so you can get those lovely looking grill marks everyone knows and loves.
5. Grill your chops for three more minutes.
6. Flip your pork chops now, and then continue with the grilling, until the internal temperature of the pork chops hits 145 degrees Fahrenheit, which should happen in about 6 to 8 minutes more.
7. You'll find that brined pork chops will be much faster to cook than unbrined chops, so do monitor the temperature on the inside.
8. Tent your pork chops for about 5 minutes.
9. Serve it up and enjoy!

A little something to keep in mind: You're going to need a pigtail food flipper, if you want to rotate your meat. That is a much better option than a pair of tongs, as you don't want to risk using way more pressure than you need when you pinch the pork chops to flip them. That alone might make a lot of the sweet, succulent juices to escape, and we don't want that.

Chapter Eight: Seafood

Oh, how I love seafood! There's nothing quite like it, whether we're talking about shrimps, oysters, crabs, or any of the bajillion delicious tasting fishes out there! So let's get started with a recipe that's sure to leave you satisfied!

Alder Creole Wild Pacific Rockfish

The Pacific rockfish is a category that comprises of more than 70 various kinds of fish similar to bass. You can find them in abundance along the west coast of North America. Rockfish are rather lean, mildly flavored, and firm. It's the best kind of fish for frying and baking, as well as — you guessed it — smoking! You're going to love this one.

Servings: 4 adult sized humans

Prep time: 15 mins

Cook time: 90 mins

Rest time: 5 mins

Best pellets: alder

Ingredients

4 - 6 wild Pacific rockfish fillets (4 - 6 ounces)

2 tablespoons creole seafood seasoning

3 teaspoons olive oil (roasted, garlic flavored, extra-virgin)

Grill Prep

1. Generously coat each side of your fillets with some olive oil by rubbing it.
2. Generously dust each side with some of your creole seafood seasoning.

On The Grill

1. Set up your wood pellet smoker grill so it's ready for indirect cooking
2. Preheat your wood pellet smoker grill to 225 degrees Fahrenheit, with alder wood pellets.
3. Grab a Teflon-coated fiberglass mat, and then set your fillets on them, so that they don't stick to your rill gates as you cook.
4. Smoke your fillets until they hit an internal temperature of 140 degrees Fahrenheit. That should take about 90 minutes.
5. Now allow your fillets to rest after all that smoking for about 5 minutes.
6. Serve them up and enjoy some fun, fishy flavor!

A little something to keep in mind: If you want to, you could bake the fillet with your wood pellet smoker grill, using your Teflon-coated fiberglass mat. Do so at 350 degrees Fahrenheit for 25 minutes to 40 minutes. You want the internal temp to hit 140 degrees Fahrenheit. You'll know it's ready when you can easily flake off the flesh with a fork.

Hot Smoked Teriyaki Tuna

Are you ready for some amazing flavor? Well, here it comes! The idea behind this recipe is to get the same affects you would get if you were cooking with the cold smoking method. When you cold smoke your meats and all, you do so at temperatures which are below 100 degrees Fahrenheit. It's a bit of a challenge to cold smoke your food if your wood pellet smoker grill does not have a separate compartment for cold smoking, as most wood pellet smoker grills do not go below 170 degrees Fahrenheit. So you might want to consider getting a wood pellet smoker grill like the MAK Grills 2 Star Super Smoker Box. For this recipe, we're using tuna, but you can use other kinds of fish like halibut, salmon, and Pacific rockfish.

Serving: 4 adult sized humans

Prep time: 5 - 7 hours (that's 3 hours or brining, and 2 - 4 for drying)

Cook time: 2 hours

Rest time: 10 mins

Best pellets: alder

Ingredients

2 fresh tuna steaks (10 ounces)

2 cups teriyaki marinade sauce

Grill Prep

1. As uniformly as you can, slice your tuna into slices that are 2 inches thick.
2. Grab a 1-gallon sealable plastic baggie, and then put your tuna in it, as well as the marinade.
3. Put the baggie in a shallow baking dish, which will keep any leak contained.
4. Let that sit in your fridge for 3 hours. Each hour, you must rotate the tuna.
5. Once the 3 hours have elapsed, take the tuna out of the marinade, and then as lightly as possible, use a paper towel to pat it dry.
6. Now let your tuna air-dry for a bit, in your fridge, uncovered. This will take about 2 to 4 hours. You'll know it's all done when you see pellicles begin to form.

On The Grill

1. Set up your wood pellet smoker grill so that it's ready for indirect cooking.
2. Preheat your wood pellet smoker grill to 180 degrees Fahrenheit, using alder wood pellets.
3. Set your tuna on your Teflon-coated fiberglass mat, or if you wish, you could set the tuna right on your grill graters. Smoke the tuna for an hour.
4. Once that time has elapsed, crank up the temperature to 250 degrees Fahrenheit, and smoke for another hour, until the internal temperature of your tuna hits 145 degrees Fahrenheit.
5. Take the tuna off the grill, and then let it rest for 10 minutes.
6. What are you waiting for? Serve and enjoy!

A little something to keep in mind: You want to make sure your tuna slices are consistent in size. If they are not, they will smoke at different rates, and won't taste so good.

Shrimp Stuffed Tilapia

This is super easy and quick to make. If you want to feel like you're having a meal at a five-star restaurant, then this is it!

Serving: 5 adult sized humans

Prep time: 20 mins

Cook time: 30 - 45 min

Rest time: 5 mins

Best pellets: all

Ingredients

5 farmed tilapia fillets (fresh, 4 - 6 ounces)

1 ½ teaspoons smoked paprika

2 tablespoons olive oil (extra virgin)

1 ½ teaspoons seafood seasoning

For shrimp stuffing:

1 pound shrimp (peeled, deveined, detailed, cooked)

1 tablespoon butter (salted)

1 cup red onion (finely diced)

1 cup Italian breadcrumbs

½ cup mayonnaise

2 teaspoons parsley (fresh and chopped, or dried)

1 egg (large, beaten)

1 ½ teaspoons Fagundes Famous Seasoning, or salt and pepper to taste

Grill Prep

1. Chop the shrimp as finely as possible, using a salsa maker, a food processor, or a knife.
2. Grab a small skillet and set it on the fire, medium-high heat. Melt your butter, and then toss in your red onion. Sauté till translucent. This should take 3 minutes. Set it aside to cool to room temp.
3. Mix your shrimp, sautéed onion, and the rest of the ingredients in a big bowl.
4. Cover it all up and keep it in your fridge until it's time to use it. Always consume shrimp stuffing within two days of making it.
5. Grab your fillets, and slather both sides with some olive oil.
6. Take ⅓ cup of your stuffing and spoon it on the back side of your fillets. You'll know the back by its reddish stripping.
7. With a spoon, make your stuffing flatten out against the bottom part of your fillet.
8. Fold your tilapia in half, and then using 2 toothpicks or more, secure your fish.

On The Grill

1. Set up your wood pellet smoker grill so that it's ready for indirect cooking.
2. Preheat your wood pellet smoker grill to 400 degrees Fahrenheit, with whatever wood pellets you want.
3. Grab a nonstick grilling tray, and set your stuffed fillets on it.
4. Put the tray on the grill, and then bake your tilapia for 30 minutes to 45 minutes, or your probe tells you they have hit an internal temperature of 145 degrees Fahrenheit, and you can flake your fish easily with a fork.
5. Rest the fish for 5 minutes.
6. Serve and enjoy!

A little something to keep in mind: The amount of time your spend cooking will depend on just how thick your fillets are. You definitely want to keep a nonstick grilling tray handy, when you're working with fish and veggies. You can use the leftover shrimp stuffing later to make some awesome recipes like shrimp cake hor d'oeuvre. To do that, take ⅓ cup of stuffing, create thin patties out of them, and then fry them for just a few minutes with some vegetable oil or olive oil. Not bad!

Chapter Nine: Vegetables

No cookbook worth its salt could possibly not talk about vegetable recipes! So let's begin right away.

Grilled Zucchini Squash Spears

Serving: 4 - 6 adult sized humans

Prep time: 5 mins

Cook time: 10 mins

Best pellets: oak

Ingredients

4 zucchini (medium)

2 tablespoons olive oil

1 tablespoon cherry vinegar

2 sprigs thyme (leaves pulled)

Salt and pepper to taste

Grill Prep

1. Clean your zucchini, then cut the ends off.
2. Cut each zucchini in half, and then cut the halves into thirds.

3. Grab a medium sealable plastic baggie, and then mix the rest of the ingredients in it. Throw in the zucchini as well, and toss it properly.

On The Grill

1. Set up your wood pellet smoker grill for indirect cooking.
2. Preheat your wood pellet smoker grill to 350 degrees Fahrenheit, with the lid closed. Do this for 15 minutes.
3. Take the zucchini from the bag, and then set them right on your grill grates with the cut side facing downwards.
4. Cook each side of the zucchini for 3 to 4 minutes. You want your zucchini to be nice and tender, and to have grill marks on them.
5. Take them off the grill, and then garnish with some more thyme leaves, if you like.
6. Serve and enjoy!

Smoked Pickled Green Beans

Serving: 4 - 6 adult sized humans

Prep time: 15 mins

Cook time: 45 mins

Best pellets: oak

Ingredients

1 pound green beans (blanched)

½ cup sugar

½ cup salt

1 tablespoon red pepper flakes

2 cups ice water

2 cups white wine vinegar

On The Grill

1. Set up your wood pellet smoker grill so that it's ready for indirect cooking.
2. Preheat your wood pellet smoker grill for 15 minutes at 180 degrees Fahrenheit.
3. Set your blanched green beans on top of a mesh grill mat, and then set the mat on your grill grate.
4. Smoke the green beans for 30 to 45 minutes. The goal is to get them to take in as much smoke as you desire.
5. Take them off the grill, and set aside.

For the brine:

1. Grab a medium sized pan, and then boil the rest of your ingredients — minus the ice water. You want to do this on medium high heat.
2. Allow the ingredients simmer for 5 to 10 minutes, and then take the pan off the heat.
3. Let the ingredients simmer for 20 minutes.
4. Pour the brine over the ice water, so it can cool.
5. Once cooled, pour it over your green beans.
6. Weigh the beans down with some plates, so you can keep them all completely underneath the brine.
7. Allow it sit for 24 hours, and then enjoy!

Grilled Broccoli Rabe

Serving: 4 - 6 adult sized humans

Prep time: 15 mins

Cook time: 10 mins

Best pellets: cherry

Ingredients

4 bunches of broccolini (or broccoli rabe, or rapini)

2 tablespoons olive oil (extra-virgin)

½ lemon

½ lemon (sliced into wedges)

Kosher sea salt, to taste

On The Grill

1. Set up your wood pellet smoker grill for indirect cooking.
2. Preheat your wood pellet smoker grill by setting the temp to high, keeping the lid shut for 15 minutes.
3. Grab a mixing bowl, and put in your broccoli rabe. Drizzle some olive oil on it.
4. With your hands, mix it all up as thoroughly as you can, making sure your veggies are evenly coated with olive oil.
5. Season with salt, mixing thoroughly.
6. In a single layer, set your broccoli rabe right on the lowest grill grate. Shut the lid and allow it to cook for 5 to 10 minutes. What you're gunning for is color, and a bit of char on one side.
7. Flip it, and then cook the other side for a few more minutes.
8. Remove the broccoli rabe from the grill grate to a serving platter. Squeeze some lemon juice from your half of a lemon evenly on top of the broccoli rabe.
9. Serve it with lemon wedges. Bon Appetit!

Chapter Ten: Pizza, Bread, and Sandwiches

Quick question: What is life without pizza, bread, and sandwiches? Nothing. You agree, don't you? Good. I'm glad we're on the same page. Now let's jump into these recipes!

Pizza Bites

So good you just gotta have them all! Let's begin!

Servings: 6 - 8 adult sized humans

Prep time: 24 hours

Cook time: 20 mins

Best pellets: mesquite

Ingredients

4 ½ cups bread flour (a little more for dusting)

1 ½ tablespoons sugar

1 cup mozzarella cheese

8 ounces pepperoni (thin strips)

For the dough:

2 teaspoons instant yeast

3 tablespoons olive oil (extra-virgin)

For the filling:

1 cup pizza sauce

1 egg for egg wash

15 ounces water (lukewarm)

Grill Prep

1. To make the dough, mix your flour, salt, sugar, and yeast in a food processor. You want to pule about 3 or 4 times, until it's all nicely blended.
2. Add your water and olive oil. Now, let your food processor keep running, until the whole mixture becomes a ball that moves easily around our bowl. Do this for 15 seconds, and then process for 15 more seconds.
3. Move the dough onto your kneading board, which should have a light dusting of flour on it. Knead by hand, once or twice. You're ginning for a smooth ball.
4. Split your dough into three equal parts, then place each part in a 1 gallon resealable plastic baggie.
5. Put them in the fridge, so they can rise till the next day.
6. 2 hours before you're ready to bake, take the dough out of the fridge, and then make the dough into balls. Do this by moving the dough towards the bottom, and then pinching it shit.
7. Flour the dough properly, and then place each ball into a different medium sized mixing bowl.
8. Cover the dough as tightly as you can with some plastic wrap, and then allow it to rise at regular room temperature. The dough should become twice its size.
9. Now, roll your dough on a flat surface, and then cut it into long strips. Gun for 3 inches by 18 inches.

10. Slice your pepperoni into strips, if they are not sliced already.
11. Grab a medium bowl and then mix your mozzarella, pepperoni, and pizza sauce.
12. Now you're going to put one tablespoon of your pizza filling on your pizza dough, every couple of inches. Do this only to a halfway point on your dough.
13. Next, the egg wash. Grab your pastry brush, and dip it into your egg. Then brush around your pizza filling.
14. Now, fold the part of the dough with no filling, over the part with filling.
15. Press down lightly between each of the pizza bites, with your fingers.
16. Grab a ravioli cutter or a pizza cutter, and then cut round about each filling, so you've got a rectangular shape which seals your crust in.
17. Move each pizza bite off onto a cookie sheet made of parchment. Cover with a towel, and allow them to rise for half an hour.

On The Grill

1. Set up your wood pellet smoker grill so that it's ready for direct cooking.
2. Preheat your wood pellet smoker grill to 350 degrees Fahrenheit, with the lid shut for 15 minutes.
3. Brush your bites with what's left of the egg wash, and then sprinkle them with salt. Then place them on the sheet tray.
4. Bake for 10 to 15 minutes. You want the exterior to be a nice golden brown.
5. Take it off the grill, and rest for five minutes.
6. Serve with some more pizza sauce, and have fun!

Donut Bread Pudding

If you've always wondered what the heck to do with leftover donuts, then this recipe is your answer!

Serving: 8 - 12 adult sized humans

Prep time: 15 mins

Cook time: 40 mins

Best pellets: oak

Ingredients

16 cake donuts (break into 1 inch pieces)

5 large eggs

2 cups heavy whipping cream

2 teaspoons vanilla extract

For the pudding:

½ cup raisins (optional; can substitute with blueberries, or dried cranberries)

For the custard:

¾ cup butter (melted, slightly cooled)

1 teaspoon cinnamon (ground)

¾ cup granulated sugar

1 pint rum raisin or cinnamon or vanilla ice cream (melted, for serving. Optional,)

Grill Prep

1. Grab a 9 by 13 inch baking pan, and butter it lightly.
2. Lay the donuts in the pan, as evenly as you can.
3. Spread the raisins on top, if you're using them.
4. Now, drizzle the whole thing as evenly as you can with butter.
5. To make your custard, grab a medium bowl, and whisk the eggs, sugar, vanilla, cinnamon, and cream together.
6. Pour the whisked mixture over your donuts, and allow it to sit for 10 to 15 minutes. Make sure you push the donuts down into the custard every now and then, and keep the whole thing covered with foil.

On The Grill

1. Set up your wood pellet smoker grill so it's ready for you to cook indirectly.
2. Preheat your wood pellet smoker grill at 350 degrees Fahrenheit for 10 to 15 minutes, lid closed.
3. Bake your bread pudding for 30 to 40 minutes. The goal is to have the custard set.
4. Take the foil off, and then bake some more for 10 extra minutes, so that the top becomes a nice, light brown.
5. Allow it cool a bit, before you cut it all into neat squares.
6. Drizzle with some delicious, melted ice cream, if you want to.
7. Serve and enjoy!

Smoked Carolina Pulled Pork Sandwiches

Serving: 6 - 8 adult sized humans

Prep time: 0 mins

Cook time: 8 hours

Best pellets: hickory

Ingredients

1 bone-in Boston butt (6 - 7 pounds)

Pork and poultry rub

1 cup apple cider vinegar

1 cup beer

2 tablespoons fresh lemon juice

1 tablespoon Worcestershire sauce

1 teaspoon red pepper flakes

Buns

For the sauce and slaw:

2 cups apple cider vinegar

1 ½ cups water

½ cup ketchup

¼ cup brown sugar

5 teaspoons salt

2 - 4 teaspoons red pepper flakes

1 teaspoon black pepper (freshly ground)

1 teaspoon white pepper (freshly ground)

½ cabbage (large, cored, shredded)

Grill Prep

1. Season your pork butt with the rub, and make sure the rub gets on every inch.
2. Wrap up your seasoned butt in some plastic, and keep in your fridge for 8 hours.
3. To make your mop sauce, grab a nonreactive bowl, and mix your lemon juice, beer, Worcestershire sauce, apple cider vinegar, and red pepper flakes in it. Then set aside.

On The Grill

1. Set up your wood pellet smoker grill for indirect cooking.
2. Preheat your wood pellet smoker grill for 15 minutes at 180 degrees Fahrenheit, with the lid shut.
3. Take the plastic off your pork butt, and then set the meat right on your grill grates. Smoke your meat for 3 hours, making sure you mop with the mop sauce with each new hour.
4. Crank up the head so it's now at 250 degrees Fahrenheit, and then keep roasting your pork until the internal temperature is 160 degrees Fahrenheit. This should take 3 more hours. Keep mopping with the mop sauce every hour on the hour.
5. Wrap up your pork butt in some foil, and then keep cooking until the internal temperature hits 204 degrees Fahrenheit.

6. Leaving your pork in foil, wrap it all up with some heavy bath towels, and then set them in an insulated cooler for one hour, max.

7. To make your vinegar sauce, grab a mixing brown and add the apple cider vinegar, ketchup, water, brown sugar, salt, red pepper flakes, white pepper, and black pepper. Stir it all up until all the crystals from the salt and sugar are fully dissolved.

8. Taste it for seasoning, and add some more sugar or red pepper flakes to suit your taste. Then let it sit for an hour, so that the flavors can mingle fully.

9. To make the Carolina coleslaw, mix the shredded cabbage with 1 cup of the vinegar sauce in a bowl, and then add ¼ of red onion (diced) as well as some shredded carrots.

10. For the pulled pork, chunk your pork into bits, making sure you get rid of the bone and any pieces of gristle or fat. Pull your pork by shredding it, and then put the shreds into a disposable roasting pan.

11. Keep the meat moist with the juices in the foil, and some of your vinegar sauce.

12. Serve your meat on your buns, along with coleslaw. Have a mean meal!

Fajita Sandwiches

Servings: 4 - 6 adult sized humans

Prep time: 25 mins

Cook time: 15 mins

Best pellets: mesquite

Ingredients

2 pounds skirt steak (trimmed)

4 limes (juiced. Add extra lime wedges to serve)

¼ cup soy sauce

2 tablespoons tequila (optional)

2 teaspoons Worcestershire sauce

2 cloves garlic (minced)

1 ½ teaspoon cumin (ground)

1 ½ teaspoon chili powder

1 teaspoon salt

½ cup + 1 tablespoon vegetable oil

1 teaspoon black pepper (freshly ground)

3 bell peppers (trimmed, seeded, cut into strips)

1 red or white onion (large, peeled, trimmed, thin wedge slices)

6 ciabatta (or other sandwich rolls you like, may be toasted or grilled)

⅓ cup cilantro leaves (fresh, to garnish)

Pico de Gallo, guacamole, pickled sliced jalapenos, sour cream, grated cheese and/or hot sauce for serving.

Grill Prep

1. Cut your steak into four even pieces, and then put them in a resealable plastic baggie. Set that aside as you prepare the marinade.
2. Grab a jar that's nice and air-tight. Add in your lime juice from the four limes, your tequila, soy sauce, and Worcestershire sauce, if you're using it. Also add in your cumin, rub, salt, garlic, and ½ cup of vegetable oil. Shake it all up as vigorously as you can, and then pour all of that over your meat.
3. Massage the bag as well as you can, so that the meat is properly coated. Then seal the bag, and keep it in your fridge for 4 to 8 hours. Don't go any longer than 8 hours, or the texture of the meat will get weird.

On The Grill

1. Grab a cast iron skillet, and set it on one side of your wood pellet smoker grill.
2. Preheat your wood pellet smoker grill on high, with the lid open. Once the fire gets going — which should take 4 to 5 minutes, tops — close the lid for 10 to 15 minutes.
3. Drain the marinade from the steak, and then pat your stake dry with some paper towels, so that your meat can sear better.
4. Season the marinated meat with freshly ground black pepper.
5. Toss the rest of your oil (the tablespoon) onto your skillet.
6. Now, place your steak on the grill gate.

7. Toss half of your bell peppers, and your onions onto the skillet which should be pretty hot by now.
8. Grill your steaks, making sure you turn them once, cooking each side for 2 to 3 minutes, or until it's done the way you like it.
9. Stir your vegetables a bit, to give them a nice char, for 10 to 12 minutes.
10. Move the steaks to a large platter, and tent them with some aluminum foil.
11. As the steaks rest, sauté the rest of your veggies in the skillet, and then toast your ciabatta rolls on the grill, if you want. Make sure the cut sides of your ciabatta rolls are down.
12. Slice the steak as thinly as you can, going against the grain, and then arrange them on one side of the platter.
13. You can now pile the onions and peppers on the other side. You could also serve some of the sliced steak and veggies right of the skillet.
14. Garnish with some cilantro.
15. Wrap up your ciabatta rolls with a cloth napkin, and serve them in a basket, as well as your veggies and meat, and the condiments to accompany them.

Chapter Eleven: Dessert

Who doesn't love a sweet treat? We're going to have fun exploring these incredible dessert recipes, right now!

Baked S'mores Donut

Servings: 8 - 12 adult sized humans

Prep time: 10 mins

Cook time: 35 mins

Best pellets: maple

Ingredients

For the donuts:

1 cup all-purpose flour

Cooking spray

¼ teaspoon baking soda

⅓ cup sugar

¾ cup buttermilk

2 tablespoons butter (unsalted)

1 egg

½ teaspoon vanilla extract

4 chocolate bars (whatever kind you want)

24 marshmallows (sliced in half)

For the Glaze

¼ cup whole milk

1 teaspoon vanilla extract

2 cups confectioners' sugar

Grill Prep

1. Spray the donut pans with some cooking spray.
2. Grab a large mixing bowl, and whisk your sugar, flour, and baking soda together.
3. Grab a different bowl, whisk your egg, melted butter, buttermilk, and vanilla.
4. Mix the dry and wet ingredients using a spatula, blending them perfectly.
5. Pipe your batter onto your greased donut pans.

On The Grill

1. Set up your wood pellet smoker grill for indirect cooking.
2. Preheat your wood pellet smoker grill for 10 to 15 minutes at 350 degrees Fahrenheit.
3. Bake your batter for 25 minutes, till your donuts are nice and puffy, and the toothpick you insert to check it comes out nice and clean. Then let it cool in the pan.
4. Mix your vanilla and milk in a saucepan, and heat it up over low heat till it's a bit warm.
5. Sift your confectioner's sugar into your milk and vanilla mix, till it's wonderfully combined.
6. Take your glaze off the fire, and let it set on a bowl of warm water.
7. Take your delicious donuts and dip them right into your glaze, then set your cooling rack over some foil, and then set your donuts on the rack, letting them rest for 5 minutes.

8. Halve your donuts, and then place your halved marshmallows in between, as well as some chocolate.
9. Grill these sandwiches for 4 to 5 minutes. You want the chocolate and marshmallows to melt.
10. Take them off the grill, serve, and enjoy!

Baked Cherry Cheesecake Galette

Serving: 6 - 8 adult sized humans

Prep time: 10 mins

Cook time: 20 mins

Best pellets: pecan

Ingredients

For the cherry filling:

1 pound cherries (thawed, drained)

¼ cup sugar

1 teaspoon cornstarch

1 teaspoon coriander

A pinch of salt

1 tablespoon orange zest

½ tablespoon lemon zest

For the cream cheese filling:

8 ounces cream cheese (softened)

1 teaspoon vanilla

¼ cup sugar

1 egg

For the galette:

1 refrigerated pie crust

Egg wash (1 egg, 1 tablespoon water, cream or milk)

Granulated sugar

Vanilla ice cream to serve

Grill Prep

1. Grab a medium bowl, and mix you cherries, orange zest, lemon zest, coriander, half of the sugar, cornstarch, and a pinch of salt.
2. Grab another bowl, and in it, mix your egg, vanilla, and cream cheese. Whip them up.
3. Get your pie dough onto a sheet tray, and then stretch it out with a rolling pin. Get it to about 1 inch in diameter.
4. Spread out your cream cheese filling in the middle of the pie dough. Be careful to leave a border of an inch around the edge. Then pile on your cherry mix on the cream cheese.
5. Now, you're going to fold in the edges of the pie dough into little parts, over the filling.
6. Next, brush the edges of the pie dough with egg wash, and then sprinkle on some granulated sugar.

On The Grill

1. Set up your wood pellet smoker grill for indirect cooking.
2. Preheat your wood pellet smoker grill at a temperature of 350 degrees Fahrenheit, keeping it closed, for 15 minutes.
3. Set your sheet try right on the grill grate, and then bake that yummy goodness for 15 to 20 minutes. You want the crust to become nice and golden brown, and for the cheesecake filling to be completely set.
4. Dish the galette while warm with some ice cream. And then enjoy.

Smoked Salted Caramel Apple Pie

Servings: 4 - 6 adult sized humans

Prep time: 30 mins

Cook time: 30 mins

Best pellets: apple

Ingredients

For the apple pie:

1 pastry (for double crust pie)

6 granny smith apples (cored, peeled, and sliced)

For the smoked, salted caramel:

1 cup brown sugar

¾ cup light corn syrup

6 tablespoons butter (unsalted, cut in pieces)

1 cup warm smoked cream

1 teaspoon sea salt

Grill Prep

1. Grab a large pan and fill it with water and ice.
2. Grab a shallow, smaller pan, and then put in your cream. Take that smaller pan and place it in the large pan with ice and water.
3. Set this on your wood pellet smoker grill for 15 to 20 minutes.
4. For the caramel, mix your corn syrup and sugar in a saucepan, and then cook it all using medium heat. Be sure to stir every so often, until the back of your spoon is coated and begins to turn copper.
5. Next, add the butter, salt, and smoked cream, and then stir.
6. Get your pie crust, apples, and salted caramel. Put a pie crust on a pie plate, and then fill it with slices of apples.
7. Pour on the caramel next.
8. Put on the top crust over all of that, and then crimp both crusts together to keep them locked in.
9. Create a few slits in the top crust, so that the steam can be released as you bake.
10. Brush with some cream or egg, and then sprinkle with some sea salt and raw sugar.

On The Grill

1. Set up your wood pellet smoker grill for indirect cooking.
2. Preheat your wood pellet smoker grill for 10 to 15 minutes at 375 degrees Fahrenheit, keeping the lid closed as soon as the fire gets started (should take 4 to 5 minutes, tops).
3. Set the pie on your grill, and then bake for 20 minutes.
4. At the 20 minute mark, lower the heat to 325 degrees Fahrenheit, and then let it cook for 35 minutes more. You want the crust to be a nice golden brown, and the filling should be bubbly when it's ready.
5. Take the pie off the grill, and allow it to cool and rest.
6. Serve with some vanilla ice cream, and enjoy!

Chocolate Lava Cake with Smoked Whipped Cream

Servings: 4 - 6 adult sized humans

Prep time: 20 mins

Cook time: 40 mins

Best pellets: apple

Ingredients

½ cup butter

220 grams semi-sweet chocolate

1 cup powdered sugar

2 egg yolks

2 eggs (large)

6 tablespoons flour

1 pint heavy whipping cream

¼ cup confectioners' sugar

1 tablespoon bourbon vanilla

1 tablespoon butter (melted)

Cocoa powder (for dusting)

Confectioners' sugar (for dusting)

Grill Prep and Meal Prep

1. Set up your wood pellet smoker grill for indirect cooking.
2. Start up your wood pellet smoker grill. You just need to get the fire going.
3. Grab an aluminum baking pan, and then add your cream to it.
4. Put the pan on your wood pellet smoker grill, and allow it smoke for 5 minutes.
5. Grab a large mixing bowl, and then pour in your smoked cream. Now keep that in the fridge for later.
6. Turn up your grill to 375 degrees Fahrenheit, and let it preheat, with the lid closed, for 10 to 15 minutes.
7. With 1 tablespoon of butter, brush 4 little souffle cups.
8. Melt your chocolate, as well as what's left of the butter, using a heatproof bowl over boiling water. Stir until it's all smooth and there are no lumps left.
9. Now add your eggs, egg yolks, and powdered sugar, stirring the whole time.
10. Now, add in the floor whisking it all in, until the whole thing is perfectly blended.
11. Pour this batter into your souffle cups, then set them on your wood pellet smoker grill and allow them to bake for 13 to 14 minutes — or until the sides are completely set.
12. Now, take out the smoked cream from your fridge. It should be nice and chilled, at this point.
13. Add in the bourbon vanilla, and whip it up until it's all airy.
14. Add in your confectioners' sugar, and don't stop whipping until the cream creates stiff peaks.
15. Dust some of your lava cakes with cocoa and confectioners' sugar. You may top it all off with a dollop or two of smoky whipped cream.
16. Serve and enjoy!

Chapter Twelve: Sauces

Sauces are key when it comes to your wood pellet smoker grill meals. You simply cannot do without them! So here are a few of the most amazing sauces ever. Feel free to tweak them as you please.

Bourbon Barbecue Sauce

Servings: 8 - 12 adult sized humans

Prep time: 5 mins

Cook time: 40 mins

Best pellets: hickory

Ingredients

½ onion (minced)

¾ cup bourbon whiskey

4 cloves garlic (minced)

½ teaspoon black pepper (ground)

2 cups ketchup

⅓ cup cider vinegar

½ tablespoon salt

¼ cup tomato paste

½ cup packed brown sugar

¼ cup Worcestershire sauce

⅓ teaspoons hot pepper sauce (or add as you see fit)

How to Make Your Sauce

1. Set your wood pellet smoker grill for indirect cooking.
2. Preheat your wood pellet smoker grill at 350 degrees Fahrenheit for 15 minutes, with the lid closed.
3. Grab a large skillet, and add your garlic, whiskey, and onion. Let it all simmer for 20 minutes on your wood pellet smoker grill. You're waiting for the onions to get translucent.
4. Toss in the salt, ground black pepper, tomato paste, ketchup, Worcestershire sauce, vinegar, brown sugar, and hot pepper sauce. Mix it all up.
5. Bring it all to a boil, then drop the heat to 225 degrees Fahrenheit and then let it simmer for 20 minutes more.
6. If you like your sauce smooth, then use a strainer to extract it from the onions and stuff.
7. Enjoy this sauce with your barbecue meals!

Texas Style Coffee Mop Sauce

Serving: 8 - 12 adult sized humans

Prep time: 5 mins

Cook time: 25 mins

Best pellets: all

Ingredients

1 tablespoon sugar

1 cup Catsup

¼ cup butter

½ cup Worcestershire sauce

1 cup dark or strong coffee

1 tablespoon black pepper (fresh, coarse, ground)

1 tablespoon kosher salt

How to Make Your Sauce

1. Mix all your ingredients in a pot large enough to allow you to work without it spilling over
2. Set up your wood pellet smoker grill for direct cooking
3. Preheat your wood pellet smoker grill to 350 degrees Fahrenheit for 15 minutes, with the lid closed.
4. Now simmer your ingredients on your wood pellet smoker grill for 20 minutes. Allow it to thicken. Enjoy!

Beer Mopping Sauce

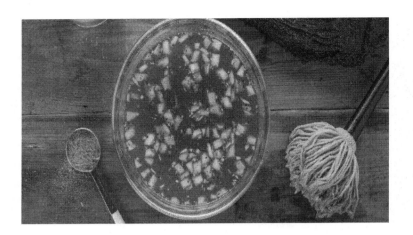

Serving: 8 - 12 adult sized humans

Prep time: 5 mins

Cook time: 20 mins

Best pellets: hickory

Ingredients

12 ounces of beer

½ cup water

½ cup cider vinegar

½ cup canola or corn oil

½ onion (medium, chopped)

2 garlic cloves (minced)

1 tablespoon Worcestershire sauce

1 tablespoon brisket seasoning

How to Make Your Sauce

1. Whisk your ingredients all together in a saucepan.
2. Set up your wood pellet smoker grill for direct cooking
3. Preheat your wood pellet smoker grill at 350 degrees Fahrenheit for 15 minutes, with the lid closed
4. Let your ingredients simmer on the grates, till they come to a boil, then lower the heat.
5. Let it get nice and thick, and then take it off the grill, and let it cool

Carolina Mopping Sauce

Serving: 8 - 12 adult sized humans

Prep time: 5 mins

Cook time: 5 mins

Ingredients

1 cup cider vinegar

1 tablespoon hot sauce

1 tablespoon red pepper flakes

1 cup distilled white

1 teaspoon onion powder

1 teaspoon garlic powder

2 tablespoons brown sugar (packed)

1 teaspoon dry mustard

½ teaspoon salt

¼ teaspoon black pepper (ground)

How to Make Your Sauce

1. Simply mix all your ingredients together, and then store in an air-tight fridge for a month. If you need more heat, just add some more red pepper flakes.

Pulled Pork Mop Recipe

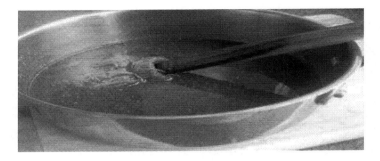

Serving: 8 - 12 adult sized humans

Prep time: 5 mins

Cook time: 5 mins

Ingredients

16 ounces cider vinegar

16 ounces vegetable oil

32 ounces water

1 cup ultra-dry rub

2 tablespoons Worcestershire sauce

2 tablespoons soy sauce

How to Make Your Sauce

1. Simply whisk all the ingredients together, after dissolving your dry rub with some hot water.

Conclusion

So we've come to the end of this book of amazing recipes! I wish I could write even more, because I have much more to share with you.

I honestly do not believe there is a more efficient way to make smoky meals that you and the whole family would enjoy, than to use wood pellet smoker grills. They are simply amazing and versatile, without a doubt.

Preparing all these recipes (and more, which I hope to share in another book) is a breeze when you're using wood pellet smoker grills, because they are fuel efficient, you don't have to deal with dangerous flare ups, you don't need to be a world class pitmaster or anything of the sort, and you can get the job done quickly and cleanly. Yet another thing to love is the fact that you can just "set and forget" your meals, without having to babysit them for hours and hours on end. Seriously, what's not to love?

There are countless recipes which crop up day after day. Don't be afraid to go exploring on the internet! And no matter what any so called pro says, do not be afraid to experiment. Unless you have to cook a meal for Chef Gordon, in which case, I wish you Godspeed, my friend. All kidding aside, Just remember, that no matter what you do, have fun with it! Don't be afraid to mix and match. There's nothing that cannot be remedied, and even then, if you mess up, it's not a disaster. It could become an entirely new recipe! If you do create something new and different, I'd love to hear from you about it!

I don't know about you, but there's nothing quite like the flavor you get from smoking your food. It's just so intense, in a really good way. The best part about all of these recipes are that you don't have to be up all night. You can trust that you can get it done much faster than, say, shoveling coal into a pit because you're trying to smoke yourself some pork rinds or something for 26 hours so you can finally enjoy a meal. You and I can both agree on the fact that that is not just ludicrous, but stressful. Thankfully, with wood pellet smoker grills, such stressful methods of cooking can now be a thing of the past.

Never again will you have to deal with the wind fighting against your grill, causing the temperature of your smokes to go violently up and then just as violently down. Thanks to this wonderful amazing device, you can actually get smoking down to a science! You know how long it takes to make each meal, and you know the temperatures for sure.

It doesn't get any better than that, folks! I still remember the joy I felt when I first discovered the wood pellet smoker grill. Since my discovery, I have refused to go back to the old way of smoking and grilling, and I've since come up with more recipes than I care to count. I think if you were to give this a try, you'll be pleasantly surprised to find yourself catching the wood pellet smoker grill bug too.

I wrote this book with all the love in my heart that I have for food. I love to cook it, for myself, and for others. I love to watch the looks on other people's faces as they take that first glorious bite. I truly believe that good food is a blessing to be appreciated, and an art worth mastering. It's a gift worth sharing to the world. With this in mind, I set out to share a few of the recipes I do know and love, with the hopes that you, too, may discover and enjoy the wonders of smokes and grills.

So, what are you waiting for? Which recipe are you going to try first? Who are you going to serve it to? Stop overthinking it and go make your very first meal already! I bet you're going to make it even better than I could ever have imagined.

Made in the USA
San Bernardino, CA
27 March 2020